SPRING 57

A JOURNAL OF

ARCHETYPE

AND

CULTURE

Spring, 1995

SPRING JOURNAL

WOODSTOCK, CONNECTICUT 06281

ACKNOWLEDGMENTS

To Princeton University Press for quotations from the *Collected Works (CW)* of C. G. Jung (Bollingen Series XX), translated by R. F. C. Hull, edited by H. Read, M. Fordham, G. Adler, and Wm. McGuire, and published in Great Britain by Routledge and Kegan Paul, London. Other quotations have been acknowledged throughout in appropriate notes and references.

Spring is printed in the United States of America, text on acid free paper.

Spring is the oldest Jungian journal in the world. It was founded in 1941 by the Analytical Psychology Club of New York. In 1970, James Hillman transferred its editing and publication to Zürich, Switzerland. From 1978 to 1988, it was edited in Dallas, Texas. Since 1988 it has been edited in Connecticut.

CONTENTS

SPRING 57: ARCHETYPAL SEX

In putting together an issue on the theme of Archetypal Sex we see more than ever what the phrase "depth psychology" means. While usually used to imply a depth of soul or unconscious probing, a vertical descent into the bottomless pit called psyche, it also has a lateral move. It has range. The horizontal range of archetypal psychology needs to be promoted more than it is.

Rachel Pollack's discussion of transsexual psyche, for instance, illustrates the complexity of that sexual dimension as few of us would ever imagine it. We all have our own sexual dimension from which we view others, sometimes so routinely, so literalistically or even legalistically, that we fail to see what a small piece of the sexual universe it is that each of us possesses.

Aphrodite's altar is where we usually make our sacrifices to love and Eros. But Archetypal Sex is a bigger subject than even that awesome goddess can contain. And as Jay Livernois shows us, our culture does not even have the whole story on Aphrodite herself, as a look at her Haitian parallel, *Erzulie*, makes clear.

All the gods and goddesses, after all, have a sexual side. While the poets used to say that all the gods were ruled by Aphrodite, they knew very well that these divine figures each embodied a sexual life of their own invention and uniqueness. Hermes alone, as any reader of the literature by now knows, is an enormous study in sexuality, and William Doty's article in this issue reminds us again how powerful this god is in sexual imagination.

The sexual imagination itself is what James Hillman is trying to encourage in his discussion of our attitudes toward pornography. He lets Aphrodite speak much of his argument, but there are other voices at work in this piece, too, as the attentive reader will surely hear.

Alan Hamilton's reading of men and women, the patriarchalist and the feminist, is as challenging as Rachel Pollack's, though in an utterly different way. The unusual is in fact everywhere once you start looking at a subject archetypally, a sign that one is into "depths" even when the matter under examination is a hot one on the cultural surface of the moment.

Thus we celebrate Archetypal Sex in this issue, blazoning the phrase on our newly designed cover for all to see, but only with the realization that our selection is inevitably a small one. Unlike the scientific or academic approach to these subjects, archetypal psychology's can never be "complete" or definitive, the whole picture, conclusive and absolute. Once again the gods humble us by the extent of their imaginative behavior and remind us what fools we are when we think our own little share of it is something to be taken as a fundamental truth.

And speaking of our cover, if you think you've seen "Pan and the Goat" before, you're right. A cropping of the original photograph, showing only the head of the god, appeared on the cover of *Spring 1988*. This time we thought, with a theme like Archetypal Sex, we could show you the rest of this sculptural masterpiece from ancient Naples. We wish we could say, "Now you've seen everything," but the point of this issue, if it has one, is that you never can.

— *The Editors*

APHRODITE – TRANSSEXUAL
GODDESS OF PASSION

RACHEL POLLACK

Transsexualism is now forty years old. Or at least the modern phenomenon called transsexualism is forty, for we can define the starting point of this phenomenon as the beginning of December, 1952, when Christine Jorgensen returned from Denmark to face reporters questioning her about her "sex change." These forty years have been marked by lurid curiosity on the part of the public, and by transsexual people themselves trying to find their place in society, either through concealment of their past, or through isolated pleas for understanding. However, as more and more women and men pass through this experience, a certain critical mass is reached, producing self-awareness among the people involved, almost as a spontaneous genera-tion. Transsexualism has begun to find its own archetypal depths, a movement away from seeking other people's

Rachel Pollack is the author of ten non-fiction books, as well as four novels, including the prize-winning *Unquenchable Fire*. She is the creator of the *Shining Woman Tarot* and has been described (by journalist Erik Davis) as "the most interesting writer on Tarot on the planet." She has written and lectured widely on transsexuality, including an address to the forty-nation Council of Europe.

approval and towards an exploration of what this intense journey can mean to those undertaking it.

We should explain here the use of the terms "transsexual man" and "transsexual woman." Commonly, and in much of the medical literature, a person, say, who seeks bodily changes from a male to a female form is described as a "male transsexual." Such a designation does not match the person's sense of who she herself is. She does not reshape her body because she conceives of herself as a man who would like to be a woman. Other people may assume this, and impose their "logical" vision of who she is. *But transsexualism is about passion, not logic.* In her passion, she considers herself *already* a woman, with the hormonal and surgical changes more of a confirmation than a transformation. The same holds for transsexual men ("female to male"), who consider themselves men despite an outwardly female anatomy.

This article examines a particular archetypal image, the Goddess Aphrodite, and her links to transsexual women. In particular, it looks at the myth of her origin, and her importance as a Goddess of passion and of the body. It also explores the possibility that this strange story of the Goddess's creation derives from actual practices in Greece and elsewhere.

Critical to transsexual self-awareness has been a search for archetypal resonances in myth and spiritual customs in other cultures and the ancient world. Because transsexual experience involves surgical techniques developed in the last few decades, many people consider it a wholly modern phenomenon. This may give the experience a shallowness that does not actually match the person's own sense of something with great depth and mystery. In fact, "transsexuality" is a modern approach to a condition as old and widespread as humanity itself.

"When the images change, the body changes," commented James Hillman at the 1993 Myth and Theatre Festival (in Avignon, France) in honor of Aphrodite. The transsexual person changes the body to fulfill an internal image of the self. As long as the image remains stunted, bound in by monotheist culture which denies its possibility, and by a lack of archetypal depth, so will the fulfillment of the body be limited. Transsexuality is a recreation of the soul as well as the body. Without a knowledge of the possibilities of soul, transsexual women and men too often allow their bodies and their yearnings to become the property of others—the doctors and therapists, the tv talk shows and formula autobiographies, the tabloid shock articles, the feminists and pornographers. For the creation of soul, it is not necessary that every transsexual woman explore links to Aphrodite, or the history of "sex-change" surgery in ancient Rome. What is necessary is that such images become known to the world. If the culture as a whole contains the images they will act on the body and the soul, even if a particular person does not know about them.

Since the modern emergence of transsexuals, their experience has been to a large extent controlled by surgeons and psychiatrists. Because medical intervention is possible to change the outer form of the body, people seek treatment. And because our society portrays psychiatrists as the repositors of soul wisdom, people in distress turn to them for help. Thus, many transsexual people have looked to doctors to explain to them who they are.

Our culture believes in causes. That is, it believes in a single vision of normality, with a cause for any deviation, and, with luck, a cure. When the Church ruled our consciousness, God provided the vision, and priests the cure for defects. Now we have "nature" (thought of as a force rather than a Goddess), with doctors in charge of the cures. Transsexual people, like everyone else, tend to believe in this ideology. They may worry for years what caused their problem, and may spend more years hoping some psychiatrist can fix it.

The way out begins with the realization that no one can cure them from being themselves. But this is a commonplace. To make it real, they may need to discover and embrace the Goddess within the all powerful desire of transsexuality. Significantly, more and more transsexual people have begun to describe their experience as "religious." Davina Gabriel, a transsexual rights activist and publisher, has written that no one can really grasp transsexuality without bringing in some ideas of "transcendence."

At the Aphrodite Conference I did a Tarot reading for the event, using the *Shining Woman Tarot,* of my own design. The first card drawn, via random shuffle, was the Lovers. The first picture shows a human and an angel in a fierce kiss. The image suggests a model for the work of archetypal discovery—the deep embrace of the divine and the human, the myth and the soul.

In such work, Aphrodite inspires all of us, non-transsexual as well as transsexual, not just because of her story, but also by her own willingness to "get caught," as Nor Hall says. She will fall to her own passion as willingly as she enflames others. Sappho writes, "As a whirlwind swoops on an oak, love shakes my heart." Aphrodite allows her own heart to shake more wildly than any of her lovers. She could not inspire love without a willingness to surrender to it. And so, she teaches us, transsexuals especially, that we cannot understand and unleash the power of desire without our own surrender.

Nor Hall writes, in *Those Women,* "Surrender to the body's desire is in itself a source of revelation." We, all of us, can only embrace our own imaginal souls through surrender to their demands. When we allow ourselves to do this, we discover who we are. Most people assume that transsexual women are men who somehow *decide* they would like to become women. The exact opposite is true. Many transsexual women struggle very hard to be men, for that is what society, and the evidence of their own (unaltered) bodies tell them they must be. A woman I know tried every male identity she could think of—weightlifter, sensitive heterosexual, drag queen, biker—before she finally accepted that she was not any sort of man, but a woman, and her task was not just to change her body, but to discover just what sort of woman she was.

People assume that transsexual women and men change their genders and their bodies arbitrarily, or as a matter of preference. In fact, most transsexual people, like most people everywhere, would prefer to be normal. The transsexual person must learn, and accept, what everyone needs to learn, that we cannot decide ahead of time who we are, or what identity we would like to have. We must discover and create it. For the transsexual woman this discovery becomes more acute, for the identity which emerges out of her desire is so strikingly at odds with what the world sees and expects. In the relationship between desire and identity, transsexual men and women teach a special lesson, for in order to live, and to make any sense of their lives, they must surrender totally to a desire they cannot understand, define, or control. A knowledge of archetypal models and images—not just in myth but spiritual practices—gives this surrender the true depth of soul.

Some people critical of transsexualism have suggested that doctors created the concept as well as the medical techniques. The term "transsexual" was, in fact, coined by a doctor, Harry Benjamin, as a way to distinguish a particular condition from that of "transvestites" and "homosexuals." However, Benjamin did not publish his work until some years after Christine Jorgensen's surgery. In her autobiography, Jorgensen describes how she (the female pronoun applies, even though we are speaking of a time when Jorgensen was outwardly and physically male) read about the first chemical synthesis of estrogen, managed to procure a significant amount, and then sat and held the pills in her hand, awed by the power of what she was about to do.

The medicalization of transsexualism reached its culmination in the 1970's, when it became officially listed as a psychiatric disorder. This has already begun to change, with the recent fourth edition of the *Diagnostics and Statistics Manual* of the American Psychiatric Association stating that "transsexuality per se" is not a disorder. Here too, crucial to this movement away from transsexualism as a sickness to an expression of humanity has been the realization of its ancient roots and analogues.

Before looking at the Goddess's story, we need to note that we speak here only of transsexual *women*. They are the people whom Aphrodite's myth reflects and illuminates. Her story concerns a transformation from a male form to a female, not the other way around. There is at least one myth which may speak to the experience of transsexual men, not as a transformation from a female to a male shape, but as a reconstruction of the male body. This is the story of Osiris's death and rebirth. In the myth, Set does not simply kill Osiris, but cuts him up into fourteen pieces which he, Set, scatters across the world. We might describe this condition as a mythic description of the transsexual man's sense of fragmentation before he begins to reconstruct his life and body. The myth also suggests the experience of shamanic initiation, which often includes severe hallucinations of being cut to pieces by demons. Isis, Osiris's sister and wife, finds the pieces and puts him back together; the phallus, however, is missing. As a result, Isis must construct a phallus out of wood, which she attaches to Osiris.

Where the transsexual woman seeks to remove an outer object—more precisely, to invert it and internalize her sexuality, for the modern surgical technique does not remove but reconstructs the genitals—the transsexual man seeks to build something on, very much in the way of Osiris. Just as the Aphrodite myth may reflect ancient practices of self-performed "sex change" surgery, so it is possible that the story of Osiris derives from an early form of Egyptian shamanism, in which people anatomically female took on male identities, including the wearing of wooden phalluses.

Compared to the story of Osiris, the myth of Aphrodite is much better known. Few people, however, have looked at the possible links with transsexual women. And yet, these links are very striking. The story comes from Hesiod. Though he wrote later than Homer, Hesiod is sometimes said to have recorded the older strains of the myths. And since the story he tells resembles other, lesser known Goddesses, as well as actual practices in the ancient world, we can see his story as carrying authority. It is Hesiod's story that most subsequent writers have turned to as Aphrodite's "official" origin. The usual etymology for her name, that it means "foam-born," derives from Hesiod's myth of her birth.

This myth begins with a disturbance in creation. Ouranos, the sky God created by Gaia as her consort, is oppressing his lover, smothering her by too close an embrace. At the same time, he despises the children brought forth by their nightly unions, so that as Gaia gives birth, Ouranos seizes the children and hides them in darkness.

To gain back control, Gaia creates a sickle, an instrument that by its shape derives from the crescent Moon. The sickle originally may have been a women's invention, used in prehistoric times to speed the gathering of wild plants. In a cave excavation some years ago, archaeologists found a curved stone blade which they took to be the war weapon of a chieftain. Only when one of the researchers thought to examine the instrument with a microscope did they find, not traces of blood, but rather vegetable particles. If the lunar shape, and the use in harvesting, identify the sickle as female, it suggests that the attack on Ouranos will be more than self-defense. It will (re)assert femaleness as a primary energy.

Gaia gives the sickle to her son Kronos, who ambushes his father, grabbing Ouranos's genitals in his left hand, and cutting them off with the right. Most of the literature on this story describes Kronos as "castrating" Ouranos, just as the god Attis is described as castrating himself. The same term is used in historical literature for the self-surgery performed by the Gallae, Attis's Phrygian worshippers. Freud, too, uses the term "castration" to describe the fear of the male upon first seeing the female body. But castration actually means only the removal of the testicles. In all these examples, beginning with the Greek myth, the act is the removal of the entire male organ. The difference is important, since farmers castrate animals to prevent them from fathering offspring or causing trouble in the herd, and we would think that actual castration would be enough to neutralize Ouranos as a danger to Gaia. But Kronos—and Attis, and the Gallae—seek something more, the entire removal of maleness.

Kronos throws the genitals into the sea, thereby surrendering or returning them to the primeval female body, described in modern scientific as well as mythological traditions as the womb of all life. We do not learn what happens to the organ itself. Instead, the myth tells us how the action stirs up a foam

upon the water. From this foam arises the perfect female,
Aphrodite.

We might describe the Goddess of Love as Ouranos's
daughter. Feminist descriptions of her as the daughter of Gaia
do not match the actual story—unless we consider Ouranos's
emasculation as a rebirth engineered by Gaia. There is an
interesting relationship here to contemporary transsexual
surgery. Virtually all sex reassignment surgeons are male, and
therefore analogues of Kronos. The transsexual women,
however, look on the surgery as something that joins them to
the world of women. Neo-pagans among them sometimes
describe themselves as "daughters of Gaia."

Some feminist writers assume that Hesiod, an extreme
misogynist, used this story to claim that Aphrodite belonged
entirely to male creation, in the way that Homer and
Aeschylus described Athene belonging to the male because of
her creation out of Zeus's head. This makes little sense, for
the story comes weighted with so much anxiety for men it
would hardly serve to reassure them in the face of female
power. More significantly, Aphrodite shows no special
connection to Ouranos, the way Athene does to Zeus. She is
not really his daughter so much as his *replacement*. The
overbearing male suffers the removal of his genitals, and from
that very act, the female, graceful and passionate, comes into
existence.

Aphrodite belongs to the earth, Gaia, for we find her with
fruits, with flowers, with roses and hyacinths, poppies and
pomegranates. She belongs to the sea, where she first rose
naked from the water. But she belongs as well to the sky, the
domain of Ouranos. Described as "golden" she comes with the
dawn. Doves attend her; she rides through the air on chariots
of swans and geese, birds known for their beauty and their
fierceness, for Aphrodite is not simply graceful and lovely,
but also cruel and merciless. When she comes to a rest she sits
on a throne of swans.

Most important for her sky connection, she is identified
with the planet Venus, which bears the Goddess's Roman
name. The apparent motion of the planet Venus (the path it

makes through the sky as seen from the Earth) forms a five-petaled flower over a period of eight years. At least one plant with five-pointed flowers is called "Venus's looking-glass."

Aphrodite is often depicted holding an apple. The apple, too, links the Earth and the sky, Gaia and Ouranos, for if we cut an apple in two horizontally we find a perfect five-pointed star. The sky is Aphrodite's home and her origin. Even if unwillingly, Ouranos sacrifices his very sex to create her. And then he withdraws, deep into the lost limbo of Tartarus—the same way the male persona of transsexual women may be said to withdraw once the female self fully emerges.

The parallels between Aphrodite and modern transsexual women would be striking enough if her story was wholly isolated. In fact, we find other images of Goddesses emerging from the parts or bodies of emasculated Gods. The Goddesses are often depicted as passionate, powerful and creative, as if the transformation has completed a process of development. Or, the God may be seen as out of control, dangerous, like Ouranos, with the emergent Goddess a more productive influence.

In Amathus, devotees of the local Goddess assimilated to Aphrodite described the deity as "double-sexed." They named him/her Aphroditos. According to Robert Graves, the Hittites describe how Kumarbi bites off the genitals of the sky God Anu, and then spits out the seed onto a mountain to produce a Goddess of love. Graves considers this story a source of the creation of Aphrodite. Kerenyi describes how a son of Hermes and Aphrodite refuses the love of the nymph Salmacis, but then plunges into her fountain. The god and the nymph merge.

The most significant figures in this context are the god/dess Agdisthus, and her/his son, Attis. Agdisthus was described as hermaphroditic, but also arrogant and dangerous (we might recall here Plato's myth of Zeus splitting apart hermaphroditic humans in order to limit their completeness). To tame Agdisthus, Dionysos ties the male part of his organs to a tree. When Agdisthus awakes, the phallus engorges, and a sudden movement severs it.

This gruesome act does not lead to Agdisthus becoming crippled, or withdrawn, or enraged. On the contrary, Agdisthus now emerges as Kybele, the Phrygian Goddess described later in Rome as "Great Mother of the Gods." The removal of the male organ appears to open the way for a full emergence of the female. Later in the myth, Kybele's son Attis attempts to imitate Agdisthus, with a self-performed surgery (though some accounts claim that Artemis sends a boar to gore him; the Phrygians considered Artemis another name for Kybele, an association which might be confusing to those who know Artemis only in her classical form as a virgin huntress).

Gender-changing or cross-dressing deities and heroes appear again and again in Greek myth. Sometimes they are figures of comedy, as when Achilles' mother dresses him as a woman to protect him from going to war, or when Heracles must wear women's clothes as a humiliation. Sometimes there is a link to madness, as when King Pentheus dresses as a woman to infiltrate the Bacchae, who discover him and tear him to pieces in Euripides' play. Or the crossing of genders is only suggested, as when Niobe sneers at Leto for having a mannish daughter and womanish son.

Aside from Agdisthus and Aphrodite, the most significant crossed gender deity in Greek myth is Dionysos. It is no accident that Dionysos should be the god called on to emasculate Agdisthus. Called "the womanly one," or "the hybrid," Dionysos was raised as a girl. According to Arthur Evans in "The God of Ecstasy," Dionysos's followers sometimes embodied the god as a stick decorated with a dress and a beard. Evans describes how women worshippers of the God dressed as men, with long phalluses, an image that recalls Osiris's wooden penis. Male worshippers took on the clothes and roles of women. Evans cites this description by Diodoros of Sicily: "...quite soft and delicate of body, by far excelling others in his beauty and devoted to sexual pleasure." That last phrase brings Dionysos to the realm of Aphrodite, reminding us that "ecstasy" takes us out of ourselves, but not out of our bodies. Transsexuality is a movement of passion and ecstasy. The body is its vehicle rather than its destination.

Dionysos' function as a "god of ecstasy" links him to the archaic religious structure called "shamanism," for Mircea Eliade has shown that ecstatic trance is the shaman's primary experience and source of power. Of course, the expression alone would not demonstrate a connection between Dionysos and shamanism. But the myth—and the practices of the god's followers—suggests such a connection very powerfully.

Disguised Achilles reveals himself when he chooses a sword over more feminine gifts. Dionysos, however, when offered several toys as a child, chooses a mirror, a feminine attribute, not just for its concern with beauty, but also for its moon-like power of reflection. The mirror traps him, and demonic forces dismember him and throw him into a boiling cauldron. Now, this story exactly mirrors the trance terrors of many shamans, who become cut to pieces (like Osiris), boiled alive, and otherwise broken down to allow for a rebirth as a new being— often in a new gender. (There is also a poignant parallel in the lives of many transsexual women, who as children try very hard to conceal their femininity, for they know that such slips as choosing the wrong toy can result in severe punishments, including bullying or humiliation. Psychiatrists who treat so-called "gender conflicted" children often lay traps for their involuntary patients in exactly this way. They will set out a selection of toys, such as dolls and cap guns. If the child makes the "inappropriate" choice, he or she is punished and ridiculed.)

The maenads, Dionysos's female followers, were described as taking on male characteristics under the god's power. Their behavior was considered masculine (as well as uncontrolled), and their very bodies expressed maleness, for they stood rigidly erect, like phalluses. They also acquired shamanic powers. They could run barefoot through snow for miles. They wound snakes through their hair without being bitten. The maenads did not alter their bodies through surgery, but through trance. They became trance-sexuals.

Shamans gain powers of prophecy. In this sense, we might describe the seer Teiresias as the very model of a shaman. His name, which means "he who delights in signs," occurs often enough in Greek stories of different localities to suggest that "Teiresias" was a generic term for prophet. Teiresias gains his powers, at least indirectly, by changing sex. Coming across two snakes copulating, Teiresias kills the female and is transformed into a woman. After seven years, she sees a similar sight, kills the male, and once more becomes a man, but now with a suggestion of hermaphroditism. T.S. Eliot describes Teiresias as "an old man with wrinkled dugs." In the notes to "The Wasteland" Eliot calls Teiresias the poem's main character. (The poet's own name might lead readers of the distant future to consider him a mythological character himself; "Eliot" is a variation of "Eliahu" which means "God is lord," while "TS" is the standard abbreviation for "transsexual").

According to the classical myth, Zeus and Hera argue over whether the man or the woman receives more pleasure in sex. Each one insists the other has the advantage. They ask Teiresias, and when he says the woman, Hera in her fury strikes him blind. Teiresias then receives from Zeus the gift of prophecy in compensation. While not ignoring the story that has come down to us, we can guess that it might reflect an older image of the seer who gains prophetic powers by merging genders and turning the sight inwards.

Robert Graves tells us that in southern India men fear that seeing snakes coupling will produce the "female disease," which Graves says is Herodotus' name for homosexuality. This raises an important point. None of the Greek stories about crossing gender suggests anything about same-sex desire, or sexual activity of any kind, other than the changing of identity. Despite stories that claim Teiresias spent her seven years in female form as a whore, it is clear that Teiresias does not change from man to woman and back again in order to seduce anyone, or to enjoy sex from a different side, but as a mystery of self.

Today, many people assume that transsexual women are somehow an extreme manifestation of male homosexuality. Either they must be effeminate men who identify wholly with women and want to imitate them, or else they are thought to be self-hating homosexuals who cannot accept their desires and so must become women to appear "normal." This assumption misses the point about transsexuality, that it focuses on subjects rather than objects. It is a passion of the self, not of others.

Queen Victoria was said to deny the possibility of lesbianism on the grounds that since women hated sex and only endured it for the sake of men, why would two women do anything, without a man to compel them? People sometimes express a similar attitude to transsexual women who are lesbians. Since they assume that men change sex in order to have intercourse with men, why would a "man" change sex to make love to women? The answer lies in the fact that the transsexual woman never thinks of herself as a man in the first place, and her "change" is done to fulfill an inner need, not an outer one.

A society based on monotheism assumes that people are one thing, and one thing only, and that this monolithic self can never change. Thus someone born with a penis is assumed to be male, desire women when grown up, and exhibit masculine behavior. Our culture attributes any modifications of this pattern to sickness, twisted upbringing, or genetic impairment.

Transsexual women and men demonstrate the in(ter)-dependence of four separate factors: anatomical sex, gender identity, sexual preference, and role behavior. A great many transsexual women (some say as many as a third or even a half) are lesbian. A similar high percentage of transsexual men are homosexual.

Consider the example of the woman described above, who tried every male role she could imagine before surrendering to her knowledge of herself as a woman. She has not had sex reassignment surgery and so remains genitally male, despite the development of breasts and round hips due to hormone therapy. She is also naturally very pretty. However, she rides a motorcycle and dresses in leather jackets, torn T-shirts, jeans, and heavy boots. And she is a lesbian, living for several years with a lifelong lesbian who has no doubt that her pretty, biker partner is a woman.

Shamans who change gender often do so primarily by changing their clothes and their social function in the community. In the ancient world of southern Europe and the Near East, anatomical males changed their bodies, severing their male genitals to take on female appearance and identities. The context in which they performed these acts was that of sacred worship of a powerful Goddess, and as a result of their willing sacrifice they usually became priestesses.

We have knowledge of this practice in Asia Minor, North Africa, India, Arabia, Canaan and elsewhere. The Bible gives us backhanded evidence of the practice surviving into ancient Israel, with its prohibition, "He who is wounded in the stones or hath his privy member cut off shalt not be admitted into the congregation of the Lord." (Deut. 23, 2) The Bible tends to prohibit whatever belonged to the competing religion of Goddess worship (such as the commandment against planting trees in sacred places). Indeed, Rabbi J. H. Hertz, in a commentary on this passage, wrote, "The first to be excluded are the self-mutilated or the unsexed in the service of some heathen cult."

The most documented version of these sex-changing priestesses are the Gallae, the Phrygian worshippers of Cybele who accompanied their Goddess to Rome. Accompanied by dancing and chanting, and in states of ecstasy, the Gallae initiates would "unsex" themselves, using stone sickles, an instrument which not only recalls Ouranos, but also points back to the prehistoric times. They then ran through the streets, throwing the severed genitals into doorways held open for them. The offering was considered a blessing by the household which received it, and in return they would nurse the Galla back to health. When healed, the Galla ceremoniously received women's clothes, and, dressed as a bride, entered the service of her Goddess.

The Romans displayed ambivalent attitudes to the Gallae. While some despised them, calling them eunuchs, or "drones," others, such as the poet Catullus, treated them with respect.

There is little doubt that they considered themselves to be women, or that their preeminent place on Cybele's worship derived from their changing sex. Some modern feminists, such as Merlin Stone, have suggested that the emerging patriarchy created the Gallae as substitutes for women priestesses, as a way to claim the Goddess for males. The evidence, however, supports almost the opposite. The Gallae, and their counterparts in other cultures, belong to a strain of religion very ancient and deeply embedded in the worship of mother Goddesses. Their presence deeply disturbed patriarchal consciousness, as shown in the Hebrew prohibition. Roman law forbade any non-Phrygian males from becoming Gallae.

The archaic practices continue even today, in India, with Goddess worshippers known as Hijras (the name recalls "Phrygia," though I do not know of any research connecting the two). The Hijras remove their male organs in surgery performed by a "*dai ma,*" usually a leader, or guru, in the local Hijra community. Before the British outlawed the practice in 1888, the surgery was performed in temples of the Goddess Bahuchera, a variant of Durga. The initiated Hijra, while healing, eats a diet similar to that of women after childbirth. When healed, she receives women's clothes, sometimes bridal dress, like the Gallae. Hijras dress as women, and many describe themselves as women, though outsiders will often consider them a third, or neuter sex, because they cannot bear children. Whatever their original religious function, they now perform at festivals and weddings, where they bless the bridegroom. They are popularly thought to have the power to cause impotence in men. Interestingly, when the Greek mortal Anchises discovers that his mysterious lover is in fact Aphrodite he begs her not to make him impotent. A more positive connection to the Greek Goddess goes back to the time of the moghuls in India, when Hijras performed a ritual known as "*solah shringar*" to prepare courtesans to meet their lovers.

The difference between the Gallae or Hijras and modern transsexual women may be one of cultural background and assumptions. In India today, the Hijras are most often from low caste and traditional backgrounds, while those who identify themselves as "transsexuals" come from the Western-ized middle class (the sophisticated surgical techniques of "sex reassignment" are banned in India along with the cruder operations of the Hijras). At the same time, some transsexual women in the West have begun to look to the Hijras as a partial way of addressing that intuition of "transcendence" in what they have done. The Hijras, and the Gallae, give substance to the words of Dallas Denny, political activist, medical researcher, and publisher of the magazine *Chrysalis*: "Transsexualism is a religious experience."

And transsexualism is a *passionate* experience, driven by an absolute inner conviction. It is no accident that Aphrodite, the Goddess born from Ouranos' severed genitals, should be the Goddess of love, of the body and its desires, rather than, say, the hearth, or science, or domestic bliss. And it is no accident that the cross-gendered god, Dionysos, should be the god of ecstasy.

The transsexual woman knows that she is a woman in the way we know a revelation. She knows this despite all common sense, despite all the evidence of her body and her upbringing. She knows this despite all her efforts, her heroic battle, to resist this knowledge. She knows it the moment she accepts that she knows it, when she surrenders to the body's desire. For contrary to the popular cliché, she is not at all trapped in the wrong body. She lives in exactly the *right* body, though she may be trapped in the wrong culture, with its insistence that her knowledge is either a sickness or a sin, and certainly a delusion. It is the body which leads her to revelation, which knows what it needs. She cannot know herself until she accepts what her passion is telling her, that she is a woman, and only by changing her body can she become her own truth.

At the Myth and Theatre Festival, Laurence Louppe said of Leonardo Da Vinci's work, "The body reveals the truth, of which it is a carrier," and further, "We know also that Da Vinci was a devotee" of Aphrodite. After Da Vinci's death, his more secret work revealed experiments performed on cadavers to explore the possibility of sex change surgery.

The transsexual impulse appears the world over, and always as a passion. In the words of Camille Moran, transsexual activist, "We were always here, we were here when the Earth was a green spirit. We were a natural occurrence in a singing world."

For the transsexual woman, the passion and the revelation live in her own body, and in the body of Aphrodite, who has gone before her, and who inspires her.

EVERYTHING YOU NEVER WANTED TO KNOW ABOUT THE DARK, LUNAR SIDE OF THE TRICKSTER

WILLIAM G. DOTY

Like Charlie Chaplin's tramp, perpetually hopping from the wrong to the right side of the tracks (until claimed by infinity), the trick-ster-clown gives us a fleeting glimpse of the process of creation as order and chaos in alternation. In the clown's laboratory of far-from-equilibrium states, structure is renewable only if it is able to make contact with its negation. The clown breaks the bottle that imprisons Faust's homunculus, and the psyche is revealed for what it is—a whirlwind, a flame that feeds on dissipation...The trickster creates form through dissolution, that is, scato/logically. He is in fact a 'scatterbrain' (in colloquial American terms, a 'shithead') who unites in the notation of the body the forces of chaos and lo-gos.

> —Thomas Belmonte,
> "The Trickster and the Sacred Clown"

William G. Doty is a Professor of Humanities at the University of Alabama in Tuscaloosa. His recent books include *Mythical Trickster Figures: Contours, Contexts, and Criticisms* (co-edited with William J. Hynes) and *Myths of Masculinity*.

I.

While writing *Myths of Masculinity* (Doty 1993b, and see 1993a, 1994), I was more and more puzzled by the difficulties that have faced the growth and maturation of a body of masculinist analysis and theory, difficulties comparable to those already produced over several decades in feminist thought. Although arising within academic gender studies programs, often there has been shadowy resistance to theory and explanation, as if there were something repellent about patriarchal omniscience being challenged by a raft of inconsistent arguments. Such attitudes are re-enforced by the strongly experiential emphases in men's councils and retreats (get in touch with your pain, no head tripping, walk your talk). Trickster voices are often celebrated, but as often disparaged by "serious" masculinists.

Meanwhile, while effectively challenging various monovisions, psychotherapist Howard Teich (1991, 1993) has emphasized the need to develop mascuine "homovision," a vision that recognizes and integrates the pairing of psychological and behavioral traits usually kept strictly separate. Repeatedly *the solar*, characterized by clarity, willfulness, competitiveness, endurance, desire for perfection, linear thinking, and goal-directed behavior that is objective and calculating, is sharply contrasted with *the lunar*, characterized by tenderness, receptivity, intuitiveness, compassion, changeability, abandonment, frenzy, spontaneity, artistic and emotional availability for dance, song, and prayer. (Murray Stein 1993 expands many of these categories, and identifies several subtypes and combinations.)

Teich questions the usual assignment of "feminine" to one set of traits and "masculine" to the other. He finds in the male twins featured in the origin myths of many cultures a solar and lunar balancing that homovision would consider a crucial step in male individuation. It is not so much a call for androgyny, as a recognition of, first, the historical suppression of the lunar, often equated with the female (or, Jungian-informed readers take heed, the traditionally-defined anima), to the extent that today we do not even recognize how frequently many supermale solar heroes had lunar twin partners. And second, homovision teaches the steps necessary for appropriately balanced development of solar and lunar aspects in the contemporary male psyche. Teich discovers in the solar/lunar twins "a holistic model of male unity, transcendent of the disproportionate light/dark duality upon which so many male-male configurations are prefigured" (1993:139).

In a conversation about a book on male twin myths and masculinity issues that we are writing, Teich reminded me how the earlier view of the anima in males has been so feminizing and inferiorizing, and challenged me to deal with trickster materials from the point of view of the anima and shadow. When I reflected upon the Hermes materials, in particular, I could see where they did indeed reflect a split between traditionally feminine traits such as being wily, scheming, operating in the twilight, and taking a back seat to the main speaker for whom one is merely a messenger, and traditionally masculine traits such as phallic bravado, logos rather than eros predominant, being at home in the external, public world of males, commanding, controlling, inseminating rather than bearing, initiating rather than bringing to fulfillment, and being typified by flashing new insights rather than by the comforting, familiar warmth of Hestia's hearthfire. Indeed, "to know Hermes is to know that in ourselves, that in another, which is not fixed, reliable, stable—and to honor just that instability as divine" (Downing 1993:57).

Reflecting upon being trickstered, I asked: What does it feel like when we encounter such figures? We'll see that in most cases it leaves us feeling passive, acted-upon, but also that we have been confronted less by the singular-divine than by polymorphous plurality, by fluidity, chaos, and change. Not primarily experiences of gendered confrontations, since trickster figures have ingredient within them dual gendering and indeed a relational erotics that qualifies traditional heterosexualist biases. Here "the lunar masculine" might represent something of a restorative resolution, yet its "soft male" character-

istics have made it suspect ever since the elevation of tough-
ness on the American Frontier and then more recently in
Teddy Roosevelt's cult of manly machismo.

That issue of relationships is central, since the male who is
fully aware of his twins-components presumably will not
make negative anima projections onto women that hinder
personal relations. Instead of conflating anima with shadow,
classically gendered as the psychic female image operative in
the male psyche, with the (same-sex) shadow represented as
the dark, penumbra-ed, primitive side of the individual psyche, I follow John Beebe's suggestion that it may be most productive to regard the masculine "anima as the emotional attitude a man takes toward anything (or anyone) he reflects
upon," considering "the anima [as] the man's spontaneous
working sense of his life, the way he approaches his life and
the way he reflects upon it" (1985:100). Not, note, an attitude
of gender, but a matter of spontaneous and emotional reaction to relationships and to all else that life brings, rather
than secondary abstraction or moralizing.

In the conclusion I move back to the polyonomy ("how use-
ful it is to have so many names," Hermes is told) of some of
my earlier trickster work (Doty 1980, cf. Doty 1993c), applying to aspects of this figure some of the insights that he
teaches us about others.

II.

While many trickster studies define tricksters and analyze
the meanings of their various characteristics, I work
here with the ways that trickster figures make impacts
upon us: in dreams, as we reflect upon the behaviors of others, or in learning about mythical or ritual figures that share
trickster characteristics. As I sketched the experiences, I began
to experience the duality of the trickster even in the progress
of my complaining, suffering work, for it seemed that whenever I named a negative, painful experience, a more positive,
beneficial aspect would surface. It became obvious that we today are still trickstered both positively and negatively, just as

the Greek Hermes or the Roman Mercurius brought both gain and loss and left the recipient with the task of making the most of the situation. Somewhat like writing poetry, then, my analytical work led to construction of pathways unanticipated, much as the ancient stone-carver spoke of "Hermes in the stone" emerging in the process of the creative work. On the sketchpad where I graphed and organized this section, wispy yet insistent lines crossed from one trait or experience to another, but I will let the reader imagine those interconnections as I turn to a list that is intended to be evocative rather than exhaustive.

1. Being surprised or disappointed by the undependable nature of trickster figures: somehow when the most opposite of my expectations eventuated, my programmatic obsessive self was dismayed initially, but then later came to insight the overall situation differently. From dismay at being tricked, to relief in being freed from a restrictive pattern; highlighting the incongruous (Doty 1991:237-38) leads to seeing the ordinary afresh, especially as trickster situations reveal how our initial expectations are so frequently narcissistic.

2. Shapeshifting when least expected, the trickster figure appears now female, now male, even at times hermaphroditic—and our experience is one of distrusting the appearance, desiring more consistency. In fact, in our culture, shifting to meet the situation is labeled as a feminine characteristic (see Easthope 1990:55). It is threatening to males not to know what to expect, how to relate to these multigendered figures, yet such genderbending as we have seen recently has taught us a good deal about how easily we are trapped by appearances. I hate to think of the number of times I have hailed a long-haired student from the back, assuming the student was female, only to learn "Not!" The consequence is that I have become more sensitive toward what differences gender may or may not actually convey. Even while conservative voices trumpet the importance of traditional gender distinctions, today more liberated perspectives are being built into the "Jack and Jill went up the hill" modelings of the child's initial imprint from mass culture.

3. In the lunar trickster we confront a figure who represents chaos, who exemplifies confusion and seems unruly or undependable. Yet we have no choice in being addressed, and most likely in responding in a manner that is troubled by lack of clarity and resents being placed in such a passive position. Passivity, because we do not control, and because chaos is always threatening—and yet life is like that, and the fragments of chaos often indicate creative potential: they indicate growth ahead, so long as we can flex and incorporate some new perspectives. Many of the world's thousands of trickster tales are related to the creation or transformation of the world out of chaos (Hynes and Doty 1993:15; as I put it earlier, "tricksters substitute a divine chaos for the daily ordinariness" 1991:238), so we are reminded of the fertile promises of a chaos in which various figures are not separated out rigidly according to the *DSM-III-R* (the clinician's handbook for identifying psychological disorders).

Already in the very literary texture of many of the trickster myths, as Anne Doueihi notes, "the features commonly ascribed to the trickster—contradictoriness, complexity, deceptiveness, trickery—are the features of the language of the story itself" (1993:200). While merchandizers still capitalize our yearnings for simplicity, any contemporary artist worth attending to covers canvases with intricate complexities either of image or implication (Bacon, Kiefer, Basquiat, Tansey). Postmodernist expressions will be the daily tropes of the early-twenty-first-century: we ignore the Thomas Pynchons and Kathy Ackers at the peril of remaining ignorant of the complex, overdetermined diction and grammars of the millennium into which we are progressing.

4. When the presenting situation is that of tricksters cheating or bringing luck or disaster, we respond in a number of ways. We have the sense of being wronged unfairly (but we may as well be happy to be the recipient of a boon, to be a winner, the opposite of being a loser). Such instances often make us confront our storehouses of norms internalized since childhood; disasters more than windfalls tend to do that, as they demand reconstruction of the whole personality. But be

cautious when expressing the heart's desire, for one may well have to cohabit with the results for a very long time!

5. The tricky, deceitful, wily nature of trickster figures leaves us feeling apprehensive, distrustful of rhetoric and sales pitches, fearful of being taken in, angry to learn that there are often poly-/non-sensical aspects to the world that we thought had begun to cohere so nicely. Our pop culture's emphasis upon superficial appearances, mindless simplicity, and clarity of expression leave us quite unprepared to deal with the subtleties of marketing psychology and merchandising; and the rhetorics of political discourse is precisely where the fewest correlations with reality seem to apply (see Kakutani 1994). Those who have been through trickster-exchanges learn readily enough the importance of training themselves to double-sight the apparently banal. Once worked-over by a trickster's smooth scam, twice shy about media/advertising/political seductions!

6. Such aspects of the message-bringing tricksters force us either to suffer being tricked or to gain skills in signifying usefully the messages that the hermetic messengers bring. Given our culture's resistance to working extensively upon the self or soul, let alone to learning iconographic or musical familiarity with our fantastically-rich storehouses of the arts (no previous generation ever had so many treasures so readily available), it is hardly surprising that a department of "speech communication" might be located alongside advertising and marketing in a huge school of communication (as on my own campus), rather than in the liberal arts college.

But instead of trumpeting simple how-to-sell instructions like the Sophists, tricksters such as the Greek Hermes and the Roman Mercurius (who were often appealed to in classical training in the rhetorical art of persuasion) may also elicit metaphoric insights that startle the recipients into action, as may their contemporary transformations in politics or education or religion. Interrupting the straightforward, simplistic, on-the-surface orientation of our lives, such tricksters guide primarily by forcing us to make linguistic or moral choices. They do not promise to decide in our favor, and we face always the possibility that incoming messages have been improperly conveyed; or too superficially; or only partially (Doty 1993c:62-63). But tricksters inspire as they give languages with which to understand and communicate. The appreciative adept will learn how to express and to get most expediently what one needs or desires. Tricksters begin to appear less as jokesters than as clever money-market manipulators who can teach us morally appropriate (or inappropriate— hence *caveat emptor!*) financial-psychic survival skills.

7. Stumbling over a tortoise shell on his way out of the birthing cave, Baby Hermes did not just throw it aside, but he brought profit out of loss by redefining the ordinary: he crafted the first musical lyre, later swapped off to his brother Apollo. The tricksterish element of creativity is even closer to hand here than in determining the external appearance of the planet, already mentioned. The point is re-seeing, re-shaping the banal, creating wealth from refuse, even re-aligning and re-making, as in the traditions where tricksters are healers.

At first flush, such catalytic figures can make us feel uncreative, by contrast with their powerful skills: or uninsightful, even guilty that we did not have the idea first or that we do not regularly have such great insights as our friends do; or that we cannot get away with such hilarious exploits as tricksters regularly bring off (many examples in Hynes and Doty 1993). But of course the promise is that if we can overcome the threat of newness and of change and let such stories strike home, we can release our own resources and become newly creative ourselves, feeling transformed because we have learned to elucidate the extraordinary within the ordinary.

8. Representing change, the changeable, tricksters represent threats to our stasis, to the going order; yet they can localize venues for growth and expansion. Hermes is often paired with Hestia: hers is the domestic task of caring for the household, whereas Hermes is both god of the highways and guardian of the entryway into the home. Tricksters deal with change and social intercourse and commerce and athletics, so that they are especially involved with boundaries and limits and frontiers. We may come to recognize even the trivial ele-

ments of *People* magazine as redemptive; tricksters send one not into stratospheric realms so much as into the garbage dumpsters of real life—the Metropolitan Diary column of the *New York Times* for 6 January 1994 carried Ciceil L. Gross's story about finding a double bass violin on top of a dumpster, and his subsequent series of friendly encounters as he carried the instrument through the streets of Manhattan.

9. But precisely in such limited situations, trickster talk tends to be extremely scatological or mocking toward law and order, indeed it often profanes the sacred: in an Apache example a trickster even teaches profanation as he mocks aspirants to spiritual power (Hynes and Doty 1993:3). In contrast to elevated shamanic or priestly figures, tricksters are close to home—and often downright ridiculous clowns (who represent the ritual form of tricksters). Jung saw the trickster as compensatory to the Christian concept of the saint (1969: §458), or to human consciousness as such (Samuels, Shorter, and Plaut 1986:152), and Mac Ricketts (1993) argues similarly that in ethnographic literature, trickster interests are antipodal to those of shamans and priests.

10. The realm of phallic trickster aspects found worldwide is met in our culture by avoidance and fear of contamination—in spite of Freud's blow to our rationalistic narcissism when he demonstrated how much of life is sexually-driven, and in spite of the actual obsession with the erotic in our media and everyday life! Indeed in spite of the fact that the phallic-masculine, the solar masculine, remains the primary reality icon in our society, even in the presence of women's liberationist influences around the globe.

Perhaps the trickster figure can help us to reconceive some of our gender dichotomies, so that the phallic does not merely make us fearful of being done unto or afraid that we are not nearly as big/competent. Perhaps we are ready indeed to speak of a coincidence of the lunar and the solar, a lunar-solar that recognizes that tricksters bring a gender-transcending wisdom that is post-heroic and post-patriarchal (as Allan Chinen suggests, 1993:97). I think the trickster's reappearance across modern consciousness (see the extensive bibliography

in Hynes and Doty 1993) is a sign of something moving in the
deep consciousness of our culture. In the performing arts and
literature this typically is no longer a monotheistic male but a
polytheistic, multiple-gendered spiritual being who brings not
a command but the message that we for our part have to de-
cipher appropriately, and to embody in a generative manner,
that is, in Erikson's "spirit of protecting, nourishing, and
cherishing the next generation, one's children, students, and
protégés...generativity is generosity to those less fortunate"
(Chinen 1993:69; cf. Doty 1994).

11. Embarrassed, offended by such a composite figure as has
been charted here, one asks with Anne Doueihi: "How can a
figure apparently so profane constitute part of a sacred tradition?" (1993:193). Yet there is a revisionary metaplay evident
in the fact that traditions do not merely suppress trickster
stories, but continue to tell them—indeed across the planet
they are used for the moral and religious instruction of children. Initial feelings of anger, threat, the fear of the dissolution of the growing order begin to phase into recognition that
often the sacred needs to be scrutinized, and indeed through
the releasing laughter of jester-comedians and trickster tales
one begins to conceive of speaking out against oppressive assumptions and regulations.

Such prophetic metaplay (see Hynes and Doty 1993:214-16)
recognizes that whatever the grand institutional achieve-
ments, there are always other moral aspects that get suppressed in mainline narratives. Usually the excluded come to
seem irrational and threatening, and sometimes only the response of the caught-breath to "the improper," to challenging
references addressed to the most sacred of the sacra, can allow
for breakthrough into more flexible and satisfactory modes of
existence. For instance, in his own context, Jesus' parables
were often "immoral" with respect to the established mores of
his culture, in particular with respect to the class of non-
religious followers whom his new interpretations of Judaism
would enfold. Although an ecclesiastical Christ soon became a
proper Establishment figure, thousands of people throughout
history have been touched very deeply by the all-inclusive

parables of the anti-establishment historical trickster from Nazareth (well-to-do people do not normally invite people from the bus stations into banquets; those hired in the afternoon are not usually paid as much as full-day employees; secular politicians are seldom regarded as more provident and caring than religious priests, etc.)

III.

Our results so far are that indeed, getting trickstered is no fun at first glance. In nearly every case the main problem involves a deceit or "trick" (probably ultimately from Latin *tricari*), that is to say, a disruption of the ordinary, something unexpected, a challenge to the going status quo, precisely something that affronts our sense of properly-constructed self-control. So initially tricksterish experiences can be essentially-negative experiences comparable to the classical project of bringing the anima up to consciousness: we become aware of what has not been conscious previously, and how it has influenced our behaviors. While its strangeness seems odd, even dangerous and threatening, we can learn to integrate its shadowy qualities, even to the extent of practicing a spiritual athletics that hefts new psychic skills now as it recognizes the importance of the chthonic, chaotic aspects that always attend creation narratives.

Is the trickster primarily a shadow figure? That is only important when one subsumes the trickster under the category of the anima—in which case, in traditional Jungian circles, one would have to explain how it is that women experience tricksterism, and I swear any woman would affirm that experience as probable if not inevitable. Or the trickster can be conceived of as a shadowy projection of but a particular stage of self-development; again Beebe is on the mark when he suggests that the trickster is the shadow side of the *puer aeternus* archetype, "who seems to exist only to test psychosocial limits," and who is the precursor of the hero archetype (1989:xii). Or nearly at the finish line, as in Chinen's argument that developmentally the trickster appears both initially as a counter

form of the adolescent male (Chinen works with male materials exclusively) and then subsequently in midlife as a post-
heroic figure, when "the Trickster personifies typical traits of
the immature male psyche. Boys and adolescent males, for instance, are impulsive, awkward, rebellious, and boastful, just
like the Trickster. Men normally repress these juvenile im-
pulses as they grow up and take their place in society, but the
Trickster traits reappear in maturity and demand to be inte-
grated into conscious life" (1993:247).

Such observations help us to understand something of the
bipolar experiencing of the trickster traced at the outset: the
initial adolescent experience is primarily one of dark excess, of
chaotic dissolution of borders that have yet to be determined,
whereas the midlife experience is one of holding one's own in
the face of trickster shadow figures—in fact, of holding onto
them until they bring a message or grant a boon. The boon
may often be an initiation into the feminine—or at least into
what our society currently codes as feminine—Chinen argues
that that second initiation is followed most appropriately by
the third in a male's life, namely by a post-heroic reintegra-
tion into life in society that is supported positively by self-
conscious fraternities of grown-up males (255-60). Not, one
hastens to add, identifiable with any actual men's club or fra-
ternal organization, but with the ideal such organization, in
which one recognizes other mature males as spirit brothers
and trickster comrades dedicated to the generativity that is
the trickster's ultimate boon. Such a position remythologizes
the trickster figure, reversing our cultural repression of an
apparently natural, adaptive, attitude—namely that of the lunar or feminine spontaneity and flexibility of the human psyche.

Such a perspective revises earlier associations of the trickster
with the lowly psychic shadow: consequently Jung's stating
that "the trickster is a collective shadow figure, a summation
of all the inferior traits in individuals" (1969: §484), or that
the trickster's actions are compensatory to consciousness,
would have to be rethought. Likewise we have to reconsider
the broad earlier consensus that the trickster represents a

lesser stage of social development, indeed of psycho-cultural development as such.

Jung's treatment of the Winnebago materials in Radin's *The Trickster* (1955, but cited from Jung 1969 by paragraph numbers from the *Collected Works*) set the basic tenor: the trickster represents "a psychologem ['a collective personification,' §468], an archaic psychic structure of extreme antiquity. In his clearest manifestations he is a faithful reflection of an absolutely undifferentiated human consciousness, corresponding to a psyche that has hardly left the animal level" (§465). The Winnebago trickster-tale cycle presented in Radin's book is a "reflection of an earlier, rudimentary stage of consciousness, which is what the trickster obviously seems to be" (§467); hence "Radin's trickster cycle preserves the shadow in its pristine mythological form" (§470).

While William Hynes and I reject strongly the notion that the trickster figure was always and only a figure of primitivity (1993:22), James Hillman gives me even more reason to disagree with the proposal that trickster materials are uniformly primitive and inferior, insofar as they are psychic materials, imaginal materials, which to be sure we misread readily in terms of the biases of causative-evolutionary logic: "Our strongly evolutional approach to events and images makes us always see development first, forgetting that in the realm of the imaginal all processes that belong to an image are inherent to it at all times. There is not merely a *coincidentia oppositorum* but a coincidence of processes" (1985:25), so that we would have to conceive of "primitive" elements coexisting alongside more developed elements. And as I have already mentioned, Chinen revises the primitive-to-developed paradigm by arguing that there are at least two ways in which Trickster manifests—one in adolescence and one in maturity—and I will argue in the concluding section that even that perspective needs to be enriched by recognizing that Trickster does not mean one thing. The figure *is* polyvalence and multiplicity. What will trick me up may not do the trick in your case.

We can gesture toward trickster-figures, yet such figures never remain at a primitive level, but insist themselves into the gaps wherever psychic growth ought to be occurring. That's what one experiences when confronting one of those wonderful older folks whose sparkling eyes (as they recount the tales of their lives) give evidence that self-laughter can be a healing reagent, clarifying and resolving. Clearly, the trickster is not just the blustery companion of adolescence, but keeps the juices flowing in old age as well.

IV.

Much of our world is dominated by sleasy cultural protestantisms that sharply differentiate good from evil across the entire spectrum of life—almost never are there suggestions that good people are implicated in evil projects, or that while projects may appear in one light, their depth meaning is another. Hence if the trickster isn't already given with the angels as "good," he must be "evil." Or, as Jung notes, even if "not really evil, he does the most atrocious things from sheer unconsciousness and unrelatedness" (1969: §473); but note that only four paragraphs later, Jung himself refers directly to the trickster's "evil qualities" (§477). And in referring to trickster's animality he considered him "inferior even to the beasts because he is no longer dependent upon instinct alone; yet, for all his eagerness to learn, he hasn't achieved the full measure of human awareness" (Samuels, Shorter, and Plaut 1986:152).

As Barbara Greenfield puts it, "the trickster represents undeveloped ego, being a creature of instinct and unrepressed, unsublimated desire; for this reason he often takes the form of an animal, i.e., a creature lacking in conscious awareness and self-control" (1985:198). To be sure tricksters are often associated with animals—the raven, the spider, the coyote, the hare—and it is striking how these are typically dark creatures, creatures of the twilight or borderland. There precisely where normal rationality is the weakest; places where we are most on guard, and yet nonetheless get tricked; and where psychopompic figures are necessary to guide souls between realms. As the "border-breaker *extraordinaire*, the trickster is constantly shuttling back and forth between such counterposed sectors as sacred and profane, culture and nature, life and death, and so on. Anomalous, *a-nomos*, without normativity, the trickster typically exists outside or across *all* borders, classifications, and categories. He neither norms nor is normed" (Hynes and Doty 1993:160-61).

The borderline figure deals with the unusual, not with the everyday, yet precisely because the dramas of borderline activities are not known until we cross those termini, the figures appropriate to borders are dark and indistinct (petasos-capped Hermes in contrast to golden-haired Apollo), or mysterious—and just at this point is situated the projection of evil onto "the other," onto figures such as the trickster. Hence we are confronting not so much moral evil as tarring by association with the unknown, or a strange contamination by numinous figures who have the energic powers to survive life in the arenas of psychic transition. We can surely be more cautious today about equating The Other with inferiority; likewise we ought to be able to differentiate recurrent and lasting significances in mythic figures quite apart from their "evolutionary" stage on some absolute developmental chart, whether Darwinian or Eriksonian or Neumannian.

Indeed tricksters are teachers of authority who nonetheless teach not through pious, elevated language but through lewdness and humor. Already as a baby, Hermes sings insultingly about his mother's immorality—but this is a humor that works "to detoxify men's anger and aggression, unlike the hero and patriarch who glorify both" (Chinen 1993:80). Hence we have here a trickster who is also tricked (examples in Hynes and Doty 1993:35-36); who teaches creatively by counter-example; and who is a sort of savior: because he suffers, we do not have to— "what happens to him happens to us" (Radin 1955:169).

Like the shaman or magician, he is unafraid of pollution or contamination because he has been there already and knows the tricks of the trade. Often held up as models for educating children, his teachings are hence "paradoxically moralistic; they preach about the norms by dramatizing the abnormal" (Doty 1991:239); watching him come to grips with sexual needs and bodily realities, no less than with religious and political leadership, we may learn a vital resiliance and adaptability with regard to the realities of life.

The realm of the in-between is the trickster realm, attended to both by challenging the dualisms that establish "the in-between" and by operating as a connector or mediator to those who must cross it. Such a figure is one who bridges oppositions between day and night, female and male, and public and private, and hence is a connector like Eros who challenges our isolatedness. And while countless trickster stories have him trying to put the make on a pretty young thing—he extends his extensive, flexible penis across rivers, around corners, and even across distances underground: "Oh!" says one female victim, "this *isn't* a mushroom I've sat upon!"— his stories teach a great deal about personal and social relatedness along the way.

So is this what is usually gendered as the "feminine" quality of "relatedness," one's emotional attitude toward life? What is "feminine" about it? How did the masculine Eros get to be assigned feminine status when bringing others into connection? (Yet masculine status when seeking liaisons for himself?) How else do we comprehend that men in our culture seldom are taught how to relate to other men in satisfying, long-term friendships? (see Doty 1993a). Relationships for either sex will doubtless be with both same- and other-sex partners, of varying degrees of intensity; yet how much our society might learn about heeding the messages of relationship when they are carried by the hermetic figures of the frontiers, the messengers who (precisely by threatening the daily, ordinary) hold out promises of new beginnings!

The figure is never isolate but always connected. Hermes is a companion on the journey (as god of travelers), and while he often appears in association with youths (as god of the gymnasium), one knows that even there it was the older male members of the society who recognized his significance and paid for all those herms. The figure is never singular, but always polyvalent, polyonomous and polynomous, multivoiced, always changing in appearance just as the twilight repeatedly shadows all our faces.

Coyote is not Hermes is not Mercurius is not Raven; yet they all are. Perhaps this figure remains eternally open-ended because, as Ricketts puts it, his is the preternatural image for humanity, "the humanist" as opposed to the shaman and the realm of the supernatural, the existentialist as opposed to the priest: "while the shaman and his spirits provided [people] with an opening to another world and the possibility of transcending the weaknesses of the human condition, the trickster enabled them to endure what even the gods cannot cure ultimately, the absurdity of human existence" (1993:88, 105). Absurd, yet the comic clown, old moonfaced Coyote, humorizes and humanizes our audience participation in the grand tragedy—which is now second-sighted as tragi-comedy (see especially Diamond 1990).

Might not the trickster represent one especially important archetype of the Self? Not as any single christic icon, but a figure of great vitality who inclusively models the *coincidentia oppositorum*, and yet is not limited even to its uroboric boundaries, who appears to us only when we are ready to change? This deity does not force the answer: we may turn away in disgust or feel cheated that all our years of straining preparation are as nothing when that gift of special luck is left on our competitor's doorstep.

Trickster as connector; as dark, ignored, or repressed emotional attitude; as a shadowland denizen not innately evil, but awaiting appropriate reflection upon its lunar facets. And above all the disruptive, scatological confronter of pompous inflation and isolationist narcissism. We must make of him/her/it one thing or another while avoiding the trap of isolating and inflating the *modus operandi* of the clown—in which case the trickster does not connect but remains merely an isolated solar model (over-emphasizing Hermes as regal herald-messenger, say, forgetting that he was also the declassé patron of butchers and cooks).

A vital incarnation of infinitely more than just fun and
games, trickster laughter echoes across the cracks between this
world and whatever follows or parallels it. Even as Hermes,
like Eros, connects people on this ordinary plane, he reminds
us constantly that while his dark, shadowy aspects may make
us uncomfortable, the psychic incursions "from below" are
not always dangerous or "evil," but may well point to the
transformations that seem death-bringing. But these can be
insighted as tricks, as revealing the ultimate significance of
death that makes us aware of telos and purpose, hence revert-
ing our perspectives to the deeper joys of the moment, and
helping us to see that "'death' is the way through the oppo-
sites...the self-regulation of any position by psyche, by non-
literal, metaphorical perception" (Hillman 1979:79; cf. 55-56).

Starting with oppositions, we end with fusion. Looking at
lunar/solar dualities, we find now fusions of temporality and
eternity, tricksterish approximations that may be all we can
trust or manage for the present moment. Such contextual fictions bridge our world of mythical presence and absence.
They are tricksterized, fictionalized meanings in a postfoun-
dationalist time, meanings that "remain projective approximations to the meanings we somehow find ritually satisfactory, even as they resist ultimacy and transcendence" (Doty
1990:123-24). And because they are tricksterizations, we must
grasp them oh so cautiously, the way the handsome ephebe
Apollo held the swaddled baby Hermes when he and his
brother appeared before Father/Judge Zeus—because Hermes
was infamously apt to let "little tokens" drop down the
starched shirtfronts of those who too self-assuredly picked
him up.

References

Barnaby, Karin, and Pellegrino D'Acierno, eds. *C. G. Jung and the Humanities: Toward a Hermeneutics of Culture*. Princeton: Princeton UP, 1990.

Beebe, John. "The Father's Anima." In Samuels 1985:95-109.

——. "Editor's Introduction" to C. G. Jung, *Aspects of the Masculine* [selections from several sources]. Trans. R. F. C. Hull. Princeton: Princeton UP, 1989.

Belmonte, Thomas. "The Trickster and the Sacred Clown: Revealing the Logic of the Unspeakable." In Barnaby and D'Acierno 1990:45-66.

Chinen, Allan B. *Beyond the Hero: Classic Stories of Men in Search of Soul.* New York: Tarcher, 1993.

Diamond, Stanley. "Jung Contra Freud: What It Means To Be Funny." In Barnaby and D'Acierno 1990:67-75.

Doty, William G. "Hermes' Heteronymous Appellations." In *Facing the Gods.* Ed. James Hillman. Dallas: Spring Publications, 1980; 115-33
.

——. "Contextual Fictions that Bridge Our World: 'A Whole New Poetry'." *Journal of Literature and Theology* 1990, 4/1:104-29.

——. "The Trickster." In Downing 1991:237-40.

——. "'Companionship Thick as Trees': Our Myths of Friendship." *Journal of Men's Studies* 1993a, 1/4; 359-82.

——. *Myths of Masculinity.* New York: Crossroad, 1993b.

——. "Hermes as Trickster." In Hynes and Doty 1993:46-65.

——. "Evolving Beyond the Adolescent Warrior: Postheroic Masculinist Generativity." *The Journal of Men's Studies* 1994, 2/4:353-73.

Doueihi, Anne. "Inhabiting the Space between Discourse and Story in Trickster Narratives." In Hynes and Doty 1993:193-201.

Downing, Christine, ed. *Mirrors of the Self: Archetypal Images that Shape Your Life.* A New Consciousness Reader. Los Angeles: Tarcher, 1991.

——. *Gods in Our Midst. Mythological Images of the Masculine: A Woman's View.* New York: Crossroad, 1993.

Easthope, Anthony. *What a Man's Gotta Do: The Masculine Myth in Popular Culture.* 2nd ed. Boston: Unwin Hyman, 1990 [1986].

Greenfield, Barbara. "The Archetypal Masculine: Its Manifestation in Myth, and Its Significance for Women." In Samuels 1983:187-210.

Hillman, James. *The Dream and the Underworld*. New York: HarperCollins, 1979.

——. *Anima: An Anatomy of a Personified Notion*. With excerpts from the writings of C. G. Jung and original drawings by Mary Vernon. Dallas: Spring Publications, 1985.

Hynes, William J., and William G. Doty, eds. *Mythical Trickster Figures: Contours, Contexts, and Criticisms*. Tuscaloosa: Alabama UP, 1993.

Jung, C. G. "On the Psychology of the Trickster-Figure." In Jung, *Four Archetypes: Mother, Rebirth, Spirit, Trickster* [reprinting materials from *Collected Works* 9/1, whose numbers are cited here]. Trans. R. F. C. Hull. Princeton: Princeton UP, 1969 [1954].

Kakutani, Michiko. "Opinion vs. Reality In an Age of Pundits and Spin Doctors." The *New York Times* Living Arts section, 28 January1994:B1, B10.

Radin, Paul. 1955. *The Trickster: A Study in American Indian Mythology*. With contributions by Karl Kerényi and C. G. Jung. New York: Schocken, 1955.

Ricketts, Mac Linscott. "The Shaman and the Trickster." In Hynes and Doty 1993:87-105.

Samuels, Andrew, ed. *The Father: Contemporary Jungian Perspectives*. New York: New York UP, 1985.

——; Bani Shorter; and Fred Plaut, eds. *A Critical Dictionary of Jungian Analysis*. New York: Routledge, 1986.

Stein, Murray. *Solar Conscience, Lunar Conscience: An Essay on the Psychological Foundations of Morality, Lawfulness, and the Sense of Justice*. Wilmette: Chiron, 1993.

Teich, Howard. "The Twins: An Archetypal Perspective." In Downing 1991:124-32.

——. "Homovision: The Solar/Lunar Twin-Ego." *Same-Sex Love and the Path to Wholeness*. Eds. R. H. Hopcke, K. L. Carrington, and S. Wirth. Boston: Shambhala, 1993; 136-50.

PINK MADNESS

or

Why Does Aphrodite Drive Men Crazy with Pornograhy?

JAMES HILLMAN

"Now, you will agree that to prefer the soft to what is hard is
proof enough of...Eros"
—Plato, *Symposium*, 195d

I. Aphrodite's Complaint

If you had been put in a closet for hundreds of years by
priests, philosophers and prudish women who loved their
religions more than their bodies, what would you do to
let mortals know that you are still vibrantly alive and well?
And if you were banned from actual life, except for occasional

James Hillman is the Senior Editor of this journal. Parts of this essay were
given at the Festival of Archetypal Psychology, Notre Dame, Indiana, July
1992; other parts during the Myth and Theatre Festival celebrating Aphrodite, in Villeneuve lez Avignon, France, August, 1993; and in three lec-
tures in Berkeley, California, Omaha, Nebraska, and New York City,
1994. The author is grateful to his hosts on all these occasions.

opportunities in certain circles dedicated to you or at specified
times or occupations, finding no societal frame in which to fit
into the literal realities of medieval piety, reformational capi-
talism, iron-age industrialism, ceremonial colonialism, scientific progressivism (as it transformed into therapeutic salva-
tionalism)—if there simply was no dignified place for you in
the big literal world, what avenue would be left except fantasy?

Remember, this lady's terrain is the evocation of desire, the
provocation of attraction, the invocation to pleasure. But long
hair is not allowed on the production line. Gets caught in the
cogs. Botticelli's lovely lady would have to wear a white hygi-
enic cap. Managerial women cover the pulses of throat with
high collars, like clergy. Skin shall be covered to protect from
cancer. Toes shod; nails clipped. Musty odors of the warm-
bathed flesh astringently banned with deodorants that last all
day into the sweet hours, *cinq a sept*.

To raft the wild waters with Artemis is OK; to bring a present home for Hera is OK; to plan strategy against competitors
with Athene is OK; and so too to jog with Hercules for mus-
cle tone and circulation to defeat Geras, old age. OK. Remember social Darwinism says survival of the *fittest*, not of
the loveliest. So, I, ruler of beauty and desire, how do I bring
my cosmos into the actual world where the gestures I provoke
are called sexual harassment, the lust I instigate called date
rape, the body I make concupiscible called a mere sex-object,
and the images that pullulate from my teeming greenhouse of
erotic imagination called pornography? What shall I do? Well,
she said, I have my method: I shall make men crazy; I shall
afflict them with pink madness.

By crazy I do not mean insane, violent, deluded, paranoid. I
mean crazy as cracked: crack the veneer, crack the containment in correct frameworks. Breakdown as breakthrough.
And by *pink* madness I mean putting on rose-tinted glasses to
see allure in the flesh, the aurora in the vulva, *hortus inclusus,
rosa vulva, fons et origo, cunnus mystica, fons et puteus, rosa
mystica*. Pornography shall be my path—the path of libidinal
forbidden fantasy.

I shall invade every nook of the contemporary world that has so refused me for so long with a pink madness. I shall pornographize your cars and food, your ads and vacations, your books and films, your schools and your families. I shall be unstoppable. I'll get into your T-shirts and underwear, even into your diapers, into teenie boppers, their slogans and songs, and into the old old ladies and gents in retirement colonies, on walkers in San Diego and Miami Beach. I'll show you—by *showing*, until your minds are fuzzed pink with romantic desires, with longings to getaway—trysts, nests, sweets. That is, the civilization will be crazed to get into my preserve, my secret garden. I will excite your entire culture so that even those attempting to cure their neuroses, as well as their sober psychoanalysts, will have nothing better to talk about than desire, *jouissance*, seductions, incest, molestations and the gaze into the mirror. Remember: what you call advertising, I call fantasy.

Oh, it wasn't always this way. I wasn't always excluded. Rome was *my* city, founded by my son, Aeneas; and Paris has a name like that of that wise boy who saw my beauty. Troy, too, was my city. New Orleans, Kyoto, Shiraz, Venice. No, it wasn't always as it is today. I once had plenty of room in the daily world until those fanatic martyrs took over with their nails and thorns and burlap suits, and those rabbis with their wondrous words and woolly hats. But now that I am driven from the public realm, I shall rule what has been left to me, the private, the privy secrets, the privates.

So let's start talking of the privates, and I shall let the lead go to one of my sons, not Aeneas, the hero; not Hermaphrodite, whom I conceived with Hermes; and not Eros, but another son, disfavored and disproportioned, Priapos.[1] I ask him to take the lead now, since the incantation of him, celebration of him, attempt to erect him from neglect is a principal aim of pornography. It is the figure of Priapos that makes pornography and the contention about it so fascinating.

(Fascination is the right word, since *fascinum* was a standard Roman term for the male member, as amulet, gesture, graffito, or clay trinket, to ward off evil and bring good luck.

About the evil to be warded off and the good luck to be invited—we'll speak shortly.)

First, more about our leader, my son Priapos. Several facts— the kinds scholars use to suppress me by their scholarly distancing. Priapos was, they like to say, a God of fertility. He played a "role in nearly all mysteries," says that conservative and distinguished classical scholar, Walter Burkert.[2] Processions with huge *phalloi* were the most public form of Dionysian worship. The priapic was a way to honor Dionysos and even to represent him. Since (as Heraclitus says) Dionysos and Hades are the same, the *phallos* triumphant belongs as well to Hades, and therefore has a sub-text, an intention below what is blatantly exhibited.

Something mysterious goes on during arousal. Since pornography aims at arousal, it must also have an underworld meaning of mystery and not merely an underworld meaning of criminality. Or, perhaps we must accept that both underworlds go together—the mysterious and the criminal. The very subject, pornography, let alone its images, disturbs our conventional reason because pornography invites both Dionysian ecstatic vitality and Hades's rape and death. The erected *phallos* acts as a fascinating emblem of both desire and terror.

Of course humans are never able to state just what *is* pornography. Even the august United States Supreme Court cannot speak of it clearly. As Heraclitus also said, omens and oracular mysteries do not speak clearly; they give only signs, because "nature loves to hide" (Heraclitus). Even if arousal and erection speak loud and clear, the epiphanic nature of the arousal remains mysterious, rising as it does from a bed of images. That's why sexual imagery plays such a vivid role in mystery cults and why sexual imagery fertilizes creativity (by which I mean any originating impulse). Arousal is at the origin of life and like all origins is fundamentally concealed from the clarity of understanding. We can never know how anything started. All beginnings are fantasies...maybe, even, sexual fantasies. Am I saying that the world begins in pornography?[3]

So there is a mystery to this day about the *phallos* in the basket and the rape of Persephone. These sexual and violating images were central to the Eleusinian cult that lasted as the major religious devotion of the Mediterranean for at least a thousand years. So, too, the sadistic-eroticism of the Villa dei Misteri in Pompeii. Not a virgin birth and an immaculate conception—a *phallos* in a basket! Why the porn imagery, the rape, the *phallos* at the heart of these cults which were mainly mysteries for women? What was going on?

Perhaps the mysterious moral was Aphroditic. Maybe these cults were saying, especially to women so easily captured by Hera and Hestia, by Artemis, Athene and Demeter: Women— keep sexual fantasy alive! Imagine! Imagine! Imagine! At the heart core is a hardcore porn image—a *membrum virile*. Keep lust awake in your mind—or as in India, deck the parts with boughs of flowers, bring them oils, tribute, tapers, coins. Don't lose your sexual erotic imagination. That's what "fertility" as the scholars call it really means. Keep your fantasy fertile. Don't cave in to sexual shames and secular fears about disease, abortion and menopause.

All that I am revealing to you comes from her, what she told me, much as the voice of a lady philosopher consoled Boethius in his prison cell and as Diotima spoke with Socrates about the nature of Eros. So, I am recounting what she—I hope it was she, Aphrodite[4]—indicated to me, a retired psychoanalytic man who saw hundreds and hundreds of dreams and fantasies and obsessional thoughts that we call pornographic in the psyches of what are called "patients," i.e., those humans so often suffering from the absence of Aphrodite in their actual lives and therefore victims to her incursions and her revenges.

To go on with her appeal. I am not happy, she said, and it is my nature to be happy. No, I am not happy allowed only this one access of fantasy, so I am a bit spiteful, revengeful. After all, my sister, or half-sister, was named Nemesis, and Nemesis or Retribution and I are linked closely; where I come into a human's fate Nemesis usually comes, bringing some sort of retributive justice. For instance, Paris rightly preferred me to

Athene and Hera—and out of that came terrible marvelous retribution: the Trojan War and Homer. So, pink madness is my retribution. My avenue of return.

I do want to tell you more about my extraordinary boy, Priapos, or my boy with the extraordinary equipment; actually not a boy now, but a rather heavy-set, balding, ruddy, bearded, full-grown man—though for me he will always be my boy.

According to some tales, Priapos was a "brother" of Hermaphroditos. Both were said to be offspring of Hermes and Aphrodite. But others say Priapos was sired by Dionysos; some tales say even by Zeus, directly. Finding the Father is never easy—even among the Gods. And whom am I to tell, even if I knew! Whoever the lucky father was who had the pleasure of Aphrodite's bed and body, Priapos is definitely *her* son.

Aphrodite is always there, as a mother is always there in her son. Whenever, wherever Priapos raises his balding head, Aphrodite is also there. This suggests, vulgar as it may seem to those who cling to prissy pretty sex, every hard-on is mothered by Aphrodite and is somehow carrying out her intentions, her fantasies, as the mother instigates and inspires the activities of her sons.

Of course, as the stories go, Aphrodite was horrified by her well-hung baby boy. So hung up was she on *her* notions of beauty, that she saw his body as deformity. She could not bear the sight of him. Isn't this interesting, the intolerance of excess by Aphroditic criteria of beauty. There is a lesson here for all you worshipers of the shapely, perfect, lovely, smooth and pleasing ideas of beauty. But to go on: She bore him, but could not bear him, and so she exposed him on a mountainside. A shepherd found him—that marvelous figure, the shepherd, always finding foundlings: like Oedipus, and the one in Shakespeare's *Winter's Tale* who found Perdita. Christ, too, was a shepherd who saved abandoned ones, the lost lambikins, and we all go on with this mytheme.[5] Today the good shepherd is the analyst-therapist caring for our abandoned inner child. And how betrayed and enraged and vindictive is that inner child when it discovers the archetypal link of shepherd to Pan and Priapos.

Now, this shepherd is able to save Priapos, not because he is a compassionate redeemer, but because the shepherd is himself perverse, as crooked as his crook. The shepherd's God is Pan, the goat-god, who, among other things invented masturbation— panic also. A freakish figure, like Priapos, Pan lives his life at the edge of civilization, in the pagan zone, and like Priapos provides a main stream of our humor. For instance: what is virgin wool? It comes from sheep who run faster than the shepherd.

But back to Priapos exposed. Exposure. His whole life condenses into that acorn of exposure. For, ever after, he who was exposed on the mountain side, is the exposing one, the one who exposes his significant member in statuettes, cult objects, souvenirs, charms, murals. He exposes himself and yet is always undercover, under a cloak, a kind of shirt, leaves and foliage, a toga half-raised, exhibiting his erection.

As for that garden where Priapos is to be found (he is the God of gardeners[6)]: come on, don't be conned or cozened. The garden is one of the oldest euphemisms for the genital region of women (*pudenda muliebra*), *kepos* in Greek, as we use the word "bush," and images of fruits and flowers, such as fig, melon, apricot, peach, cherry, plum, and of course, rose. So, of course, Priapos is the gardener who cares for the "garden"—a task which keeps him happily occupied. Scholarship has had to cover all this up with "fertility" because Priapos is himself covered in order to be displayed, as I am doing here—and Lopez-Pedraza did years ago in writing on Priapos.

With this we come to what's clinically called *exhibitionism*. Could it be Priapos who is displaying himself in this urge? Is this urge saying, "Look at my parts that Aphrodite rejected. I need to be seen, appreciated, taken in from abandonment, saved from this cursed orphaned condition. I am Aphrodite's son who was exposed by her and so I must return by the same route: exposure of the very part that caused my exposure." Is this what exhibitionists try to say to everyone they can show their genitals to? "Look at me. I mean you no harm. (Clinically, exhibitionists are not violent, not rapists, but usually mild and timorous men.) Receive me. See, I am proud and wonderful, despite what my Mother says."

About that curse at birth, there is more to say. About the gross genitalia, porno grossness, excess, exaggeration which so horrified Aphrodite's sensitive good taste, that penis which surpassed the standard benchmarks for the standing male member—do you know the full story of how it happened? Aphrodite, about to give birth, retired to Lampsakos, a town on the Hellespont, a place that later considered Priapos its founding Hero-God, for there he was born and there, later, his cult was celebrated, coins bearing his image cast and Priapean rituals enacted. Heroic Alexander wanted to destroy the town for its pornographic excesses. Heroes seem to be sexually shy: Hercules remaining on the Argonaut rather than dally with women; Bellerophon retreating from women who raised their skirts. Even the marbles (statues) carved to represent heroic figures and heroic Gods like Apollo show modest appendages compared with the sizable grotesqueries of satyrs, Pan and Priapos.

Now Hera was enraged at the trifling of Zeus, or of Dionysos, Zeus's son by Hera's rival, Semele. In Hera's mind this child to be born from Aphrodite was an insult in its very conception because it was directly or indirectly from Zeus. The child would be living testimony to her husband's philandering, the very progeny of the very behavior which she, Hera, Queen of Heaven, was ordained to oppose. Well, she, Hera, cheated and deceived in her own style by proffering aide to Aphrodite during her lying-in and delivery. She touched Aphrodite's belly with her finger, causing the child's unshapeliness. We must recognize the long finger of Hera in the gross genitalia of Priapos. Hera's normal straight measurement creates Priapic enormity.

Priapean enormity has many Gods in it—lots of Gods. It can't be read simply—as Lopez Pedraza says. Each Priapean excitation has in it the powers of Aphrodite, Dionysos, Hades, Zeus, maybe Hermes, and so on. But in all this let us never forget the finger of Hera. This is what a polytheistic psychology teaches about any event. There is a complex imagination released rather than a simple explanation that identifies and closes the question. We get a story rather than a reduction or a moralism, and each mythical story involves another. As the German Romantics said, "Never, never does one God appear alone."

I lay emphasis upon Hera because the other sons of Aphrodite as well as her favorites—Aeneas, Paris, Anchises, Eros, Ares, Adonis, Hermes, Dionysos were certainly not misshapen. (Hermaphroditos was indeed peculiar, because of his doubled attractiveness; and tho' Aphrodite's husband, Hephaistos, was lame, this was a deformity intimately associated, again, with Hera.) Of all the beautiful Goddess's sons and lover, only Priapos was misshapen, only this one touched by Hera.

One touch of Hera and the priapic becomes "deformed," vulgar, gross. We turn from it, repulsed; we abandon it on the mountainside and call it uncivilized, pagan. ("Pagan" literally means "of the rocky hillside.") Hera would approve of only one kind of erection, that which serves the mating game, the coupling, husbandly kind. Here, then, is the authoress of the bans against hardcore porn that grossly shows erections and invites priapic erections in return. I suspect most of the Goddesses are anti-porn: Athene took sides against the more potent forces of Poseidon and Dionysos and she didn't like horny goats; Hestia refused Priapos when he came after her; and Artemis surely doesn't chase and hunt in gardens.

Hera would exclude the excessive sexual imagination so as to keep lust within conjugal bonds. It is she who makes it ugly—not that the genitals are themselves ugly. As Georges Bataille noted, and the French do note such things, the actual genitals are the most desirable and the most repulsive at the same moment. She causes the priapic to be placed outside the limits, marginalized to the redlight district, the porn shop, away from decent people with family values. It is Hera who has turned pornography into obscenity.

Now I am not here to blame Hera or to invite her enmity. I
have enough troubles in her domain. In fact, dear lady, I regard myself as one of your devotees, having done obeisance at
your sacred places in Sicily and Paestum and made notes for a
short book favoring your virtues and their importance for our
contemporary culture. Nonetheless, Hera, allow me this analytical moment of penetration into your preserve.

The localization of priapean sexuality in a red-light district
is the literalization of a mythical domain. Priapos's garden
remains outside the house, even if relocated in an urban porn
shop. The perverse imagination—and you may recall that one
of the marks of the priapic is the penis twisted to the rear, a
metaphor, of course, and not simply a physical curiosity—does
not belong at home where the twists of the imagination are to
be laid straight. Hera's realm is where fires are cooled, following St. Paul's dictum that it is better to marry than to burn.
Pornography can ignite the dormant images in the chill of
domestic tranquility. When pornography enters the home, it
appears asinine, again in accord with myth. For one tale says
that when Priapos invades the house, attempting to take Hestia who is nodding by the hearth, an ass brays, waking her so
she can fend him off. Priapos is not for domestication. Pornography cannot be safe and sane; it cannot abide by family
values. Yet, that same ass, given its due, is also central to the
Isis mysteries of the psyche as told by Apuleius in *The Golden
Ass.*

So when Sallie Tisdale writes, in *Talk Dirty To Me,* about
her desire, a woman's desire, to visit porn shops, buy porn
videos, and watch them, and when she writes of the shame she
overcomes to free her curiosity, it's not a shame brought on
because porn-viewing is a male activity exclusively. Rather,
her shame reflects the mythical fact that porn does not belong
inside the consciousness of the normal community, its domes-
ticity and conventions as defined by Hestia and Hera. The resistance Sallie Tisdale overcomes is not patriarchal condition-
ing (women keep out); it is the archetypal resistance of these
Goddesses to Priapos and Aphrodite. Is this why usual wives
don't want to watch porn at home with their usual husbands:

the sex of two couch potatoes in front of their screen. When Sallie Tisdale visits the shop, she is like one of the women who leaves the house for the mountainsides of Dionysian mysteries, women's mysteries, those exclusive women's festivals of which Kerenyi writes: "at exclusive women's festivals, to which men are not admitted, the participants said the most shocking things to one another. At the feast of the *Haloa* there were not only obscene mockeries but some very indecent behavior. The married women were led on by means of ritual play to things forbidden in marriage."[7]

I have told the tale of Priapos, of Hera's finger on Aphrodite's belly, of his exposure and marginalization in order to show the archetypal curse on the priapic, and consequently on all vigorously erected image consciousness, that arousal of imagination which pornography seeks to achieve. It is blamed for male violence, the beating of wives, sexual excesses and unnatural distortions, degradation of women, molestation of children, rapes...all this argumentation is part of the curse put on the priapic by Hera and by her minions in the domain of the domestic, the communal, the societal.

By the way, a recent intrusion of this mythic constellation in public life occurred at the exposure of Clarence Thomas (stocky, middle-aged, balding, swarthy if not ruddy) before the United States Senate Judiciary Committee. There he was, uncovered on TV, a kind of indecent exposure when he was accused of talking about the size of the penis of the porn actor "Long Dong Silver" with his female aid, Anita Hill, and there was mention of a seductive pubic hair on a Coke can. Of the many plants used in antiquity to honor Priapos with garlands was the *adiantum*, in Roman times known as the *capillus veneris* or maiden hair or our lady's hair, and "the hair implied in these names was that of the pubes."[8]

II. Images are Instincts

Sex education, sex talk shows, sex help books, sex therapy, sex workshops—Aphrodite's pink ribbons wrap our culture round. The billion-dollar porn industry is minor league compared with the haunting sexual obsessions endemic in the culture at large. But for a moment I want to move away from both politics and morality and into psychology—the psychology of the image.

First, to Jung's psychology of the fantasy image, which, after all, is precisely what porn is: lustful fantasy images.

Jung places images and instincts on a psychological continuum, like a spectrum (*CW* 8: pp 397-420). This spectrum, or color-band, ranges from an infra-red end, the bodily action of instinctual desire, to the ultra-violet blue end of fantasy images. These fantasy images, according to Jung's model, are the pattern and form of desire. Desire isn't just a blind urge; it is formed by a pattern of behavior, a gesture, a writhing, a dancing, a poetics, a coming-on of style, and these patterns are also fantasies which present images as instinctual behaviors.

Jung does something different from Freud. Freud regards the blue or mental end to be the sublimation of the red desirous instinct. The red transforms, civilizes, sublimates into the blue for Freud. Jung, however, regards the images to be the instincts themselves. Image and instinct are naturally inseparable. You always are in a fantasy when performing an instinct, and you are always instinctually grasped when imagining a fantasy. Since images and instincts are two faces of the one thing, Jung's model implies that any change in one is a change in the other. If you mess up your instinctual life, your imagination is also messed up; if you repress your fantasy-images, your instinctual life is also repressed. This is important, very important. Instinct and Image *are* each other. Your images are instincts in fantasy form; your instincts are the patterned behavior of imaginings.

If we split the red end from the blue, we get a blue imagination without vitality, Hallmark clichés as emotions, New Age spiritualized imagination without the coarse, the strong and the lurid. And we also get the coarse, the strong and the lurid as violence, a red-end instinct deprived of formal containment and imaginative variety.

Example: Some years ago at the Kinsey archive in Bloomington, Indiana, I saw volumes of prison erotics on deposit—love letters, drawings, notebooks, artifacts, crayon sketches—the pornography made by inmates and confiscated by the guards. The blue end of the spectrum was forcibly repressed; imagination under lock and key. What then happens to the red end? Prison rape, buggery and prostitution.

When the fireman in the Los Angeles fire station fought a legal battle against feminist fire-fighters to retain his right to look at porn magazines while on call in the firehouse, he was firing up his fantasy, keeping it lively, so that the instinct necessary for his job is also alive. (He won the case, by the way.)

There is a lesson here. The confiscation of the writings and drawings in the Indiana prisons indicates a great fear, the fear of imagination itself, the fear of the uncontrollable effusion of fantasy life that cannot be held within bars and walls. I need to explain this further. For this explanation, I turn to a book by a Columbia University Professor of Art, David Freedberg, a mammoth masterly work: *The Power of Images*, University of Chicago Press.

Now, says Freedberg, "images do work in such a way as to incite desire," and since, he says, "the eyes are the channel to the other senses," all pictures make us look. They seduce us into looking. The gaze stimulates the other senses and arouses. Arousal fetishizes the object. We are fixed by it, to it. What holds the gaze is this demonic power in the image, its superhuman or divine force. Images, not only sexually explicit images, make eros visible and are demonic, and so for centuries artworks have been said to lead to vice, their beauty corrupting.

Plato insisted in the *Republic* [3: 401b] that the images of the arts must be controlled. This Aristotle restated in his *Politics* [7.17 (1336b)]: "It should therefore be the duty of government to prohibit all statuary and painting which portrays any sort of indecent action."

Because images draw us into participation with them, that part of human nature for which Plato and Aristotle here speak—the Apollonic, logical, mathematical, idealized—is brought down by images and sullied by the emotions they

arouse. The body is enlivened by images, by graphic images
especially, and the fear of that enlivened imagination, falling
to the image (Pygmalion), idol-worship, addiction, forces the
higher mind to consider censorship, such as Plato and Aristotle mention.

Censorship is an inherent response to the libidinal potency
of the image, and not to any particular content. As Freedberg
says, [The] "potential for arousal immediately and irresistibly
accrues from the interaction between images and people."
Hence, all images are threatening because the potential for
arousal is ever present.

Pornographic images present only one case of wider libidinal arousal. Holy images, too, have been savaged, as for instance Michelangelo's *Pietá*, and bourgeois images, for example, Rembrandt's *Night Watch*. Defacing, stabbing, acid attacks on paintings by Poussin, Dürer, Mantegna, Rubens,
Correggio belong to the history of art; so do also the thousands and thousands of images smashed and ripped by gov-
ernmental edicts from ancient Egypt, Persia, the Greek Islands, and the Americas to small churches in rural England.
The history of iconoclasm, of fear of the image and attempts
to control it, says clearly that *all images are pornographic in
their arousal capacity*, an arousal which recognizes the libidinal animation, the daimonic power, the active soul in the image.

When I say all images are pornographic, please let's recall
that the definition of pornography depends *not* on what is
depicted, but on its effect, the instinct in the image. As
Webster says: Porn is material depicting erotic behavior that
is *"intended to cause sexual excitement"* (my italics). Content is
contingent upon effect: arousal. That's why the content has to
be circumspectly, even privatively, defined, e.g., *without* scientific, aesthetic, etc. value. Content is insufficient for definition, because as the Supreme Court declared (Cohen vs.
California, 1971), "one man's vulgarity is another man's
lyric." We do not know pornography by what it is, but by
what it *does*. That's why Justice Potter Stewart could say, "I
know it when I see it." He knows what's porn because of what

the images do to his instincts, his emotions; arousal. The question of definition becomes simply: does the image produce a *frisson*; does it stimulate instinctual reverberation. Again, the definition of porn given in Fowler's *Dictionary of Modern Critical Terms* is that which "depraves or corrupts," i.e., what it *does*.[9]

For orthodox monotheists who follow a pure and abstract spirit, any image depraves and corrupts, even a dream, and ought to be eradicated at its source in the mind. The history of iconoclasm is long and bloody (and I have already reviewed it in my *Healing Fiction* in regard to Jung's courageous insistence upon images as the basic stuff of the psyche and therefore of its therapy). The history of iconoclasm continues in subtle forms by reducing images to allegories, interpreting them into concepts and by meditative techniques which seek to empty the mind for the sake of an imageless state.

III. Censorship

Since images are instincts, censoring images represses instincts. What then happens to the vitality of the citizen?

Here, the issue of censorship shifts from one of personal expression and belief (freedom under the First Amendment) to one of national vitality, even national security. It becomes an issue of the Constitution itself whose preamble states that our government aims to "insure domestic tranquility" and "promote the general welfare."

If tranquility of the general populace means tranquilized, then government censorship might be defensible. For, yes, pornography arouses. I submit that this potential for igniting an insurrection of the repressed instinctual imagination and for fomenting curiosity to pry into what is concealed may be the motives underlying the anxious scrutiny of pornography in our times by all three branches of government: Supreme Court, Congressional Committee and Justice Department.

Notice, please that we are now moving from myth to law in accord with an archetypal pattern of the human mind. As we

move, deliberation begins to replace delight. Aphrodite de-
throned; *nomos* and *themis* to the fore.

Right away, a definition of pornography: the stimulation of
lust through imaging and the stimulation of imaging through
lust. We may tighten this definition by omitting
"stimulation" since arousal is always contextual, depending on
variables such as time, place, mood and taste. Many lustful
images leave one limp and stupified; some imagined lust pro-
vokes only revulsion. Thus, in sum, *pornography is lustful images and imagistic lust.*

I offer this definition to replace those of the dictionaries
which link "pornographic" with "obscene"—meaning dirty,
filthy, offensive to decency and modesty. Although the
Greeks used the word *porne* for prostitute, in English
"pornography" enters the Oxford English dictionary only in
mid-Victorian times when it received its obscene qualification.

Can we clean up this mess that muddles obscenity with
pornography? Let us try to keep in mind what Murray Davis
says in his lovely book, *Smut*, "that no sexual activity is obscene in itself, but only in relation to a particular ideology.
Therefore, the central question...should be shifted from 'What
sexual activities are obscene?' to 'Relative to what [ideology]
are some sexual activities obscene?'"[10]

Although the Justice Department has a National Obscenity
Unit, precisely what obscenity is remains unclarified. Mainly,
it is defined as (a) depictions or descriptions of sexual activities
or organs, (b) appeal primarily to prurient interests offensive
to local community standards, and (c) without redeeming scientific, aesthetic, or political merit. *The obscene is wholly
sexualized.* Nuclear dumps, leaching poisons, clear-cut forest
lands, strangulated seals, disfigured toy monsters, TV tor-
tures, platters of food dumped in restaurant garbage, bomb-
ing children in Iraq, George Bush walking through South
Central L.A., Richard Serra's rusty girders plunked down in
public squares, McDonald's arches spanning the globe and the
smell of fried grease—none of this is legally obscene, yet what
of this has scientific, aesthetic or social merit? Obscenity, dis-
located from its actual daily occasions, has been displaced onto

sexual acts and organs. But I have seen buildings more obscene than Marilyn Chambers and Traci Lords—and buildings can't be turned off, you are forced to enter them. Clearly our culture is more afraid of looking at Robert Mapplethorpe's photos of a penis than of Rambo's automatic rifle. We are more afraid of viewing an ordinary human anus than the assholes we watch nightly on TV.

The struggle with pornography in America is not about obscenity. It is about ideology; and, according to Leonore Tiefer, President of the International Academy of Sex Research, particularly the ideology condemning masturbation.[11] Anathema! And why? since statistics say almost everybody masturbates, probably more citizens than brush their teeth, and certainly more than vote. Why so ideologically condemned? Partly because masturbation offers pleasure without dependence; it may even prevent shopping. Archetypally, masturbation invokes Pan, and we witness his panic when the President, employing the powers vested in him to defend the Constitution, summarily fires the Surgeon General (whom he had appointed) for stating that the youth of this nation (under God) should learn about masturbation at a time in this nation's history when HIV, gonorrhea, unwanted pregnancy and date-rape plague that same youth.

In the United States about 2000 rapes occurred today and will occur tomorrow. One out of eight adult American women will be the object of a rape—the definition of which I shall leave aside. Child molestation, child prostitution, satanic sexual cults, venereal diseases—why enumerate? All too well known to you. Violent and pathological sexual fantasies have colonized our minds. We are a nation of lustful images, a pornographic nation. This is a hardcore fact. But our pornographic nation has yet to disentangle its violence and its obscenity from pornography. For violence is the enemy, not the sexuality that may occasionally accompany it. And obscenity of the nation's taste, values, language and sensibility is only minimally and contingently represented by porn. The "problem" of what to do about porn begins first with the nation's hardcore devotion to violence and obscenity.

The way America deals with its hard facts is to make a law.
As one commentator on America has said, *law is the myth of
America*. Lawyers are our priests, our interpreters of the
dominant myth that steers the civilization, codifies its practices and provides its rituals. Of course lawyers must receive
high tribute. So, to deal with pornography we outlaw it, and
thereby blame it for inciting criminal behavior. Let us remember, however, that a definitive causal link between pornography and criminal sexual behavior has never been established. President Johnson's commission report published in
1970, and the Meese report (1986) and the Surgeon General's
report—all failed to find reliable evidence that significantly
connects pornography with criminal sexual behavior.[12]

Despite these repeated inconclusive findings, the Senate Judiciary Committee deliberated many months over the Pornography Victims Compensation Act. This bill, in its own
perversely twisted way, gives backhand recognition to the
power in the image to incite desire. For the Bill, as originally
proposed, would have held producers and distributors of pornography legally responsible for illegal actions committed by
the consumer of porn. Victims of sex crimes could file civil
suits to recover damages from producers, distributors, maybe
even actors, of "obscene" materials, if the victims could show
that the materials caused (incited, sparked, initiated) the
crimes. You would no longer be a citizen responsible for your
behavior—you are rather a victim of *Penthouse* and *Screw*.

Just here we see the effects of Hera on our legal thinking.
(Does Aphrodite write laws? What kind would they be? Does
she engage lawyers, or has she other means of getting her
own?) When the "nine old men" as Roosevelt called the Jus-
tices (and I include O'Connor and Ginzberg in that number)
consider the cases of pornography brought to the bench, they
retreat to an imaginative figure called "the average person"
[sometimes called "reasonable person"] who "applying contemporary community standards would find the work to be
patently offensive."

Who is this fictional "person?" The statistically average person in the United States would be one of Hera's marrieds (or

has been marrieds), whose repressions would reflect the peer group, i.e., standard *petit bourgeois* standards. For this "person" the images of porn—as the law states—can appeal only to "prurient interests." Once the door to porn has been closed by local community opinion, the only opening is through the key-hole. The only access for a puritan is prurience.

Then who buys porn? Where's the money coming from? "Not me," says the average reasonable standard community person. It must come then from the non-reasonable (irrational, demented?), not average (fringe?), not following community standards (a-social?) persons. There must be an awful lot of them with fat wallets to maintain the ever-expanding multi-billion dollar industry.

Porn and prurience seem inseparable because, when lustful images are uplifted into archives for the study of sexuality or collected as erotic art, no one seems to go. According to a recent report, the Kinsey archives are "falling apart," the Museum of Erotic Art in San Francisco is "defunct," and access to the patchy assembly of material in other collections like that of the New York Public Library is desultory and complicated. Moreover, "serious" interest by the reasonable person also flags. The President of the Institute for the Advanced Study of Sexuality complains: "It's difficult to get enough trained people to look at all the material we get in."[13]

That these images aimed solely to arouse must have other serious ends also takes us back to Hera (or the Roman Catholic Church) who insists all human sexuality must serve a high purpose. Do notice that pleasure, enjoyment, surprise, shock, curiosity, initiation—or just watching—are not serious enough. Priapean and Aphroditic values are judged by other values assumed to be superior. Hera raged at Zeus for not keeping within the service of marriage his philandering fantasies which generated so many extraordinary forms of existence, his progeny. And the Church has ruled for centuries that sexuality must serve procreation or marriage or God. Otherwise dalliance and the furor of the flesh belong to the Devil. The Supreme Court makes all this very literal, branding a red-letter warning into the lustful imaginings of every citizen: if you get into porn, it must only be for serious scientific, aesthetic or political value.

Political? Isn't porn itself political? From the reactions of Jesse Helms and the storms unleashed whenever Aphrodite overtly invades the body politic via arts funding, museum exhibitions or the bodies of politicians, she melts the borders between politics and pornography. Pornographic materials are *ipso facto* political in that they intend to arouse the suppressed body of the citizen in which is also the body politic.

The overlooked virtue of Andrea Dworkin's and Catherine MacKinnon's lethal assault on pornography is their coupling of porn and politics. Their move is similar to mine; the consequences of the move, however, are completely different. The argument that they have succeeded in establishing into law in Canada and partly in Minneapolis and Indianapolis runs like this: Because pornography is sexual subordination of persons, the politics of porn moves from the rights of personal expression and belief (First Amendment) to the civil rights established by the Thirteenth and Fourteenth Amendments prohibiting involuntary servitude and deprivation of liberty. They further argue that as a demonstration of the subordination of women to men, pornography discriminates against all women. It is to be banned not because it incites violence, but because it is violating. Confining it to a red-light district not only condones this involuntary servitude, but legalizes a ghetto, a slave quarter.

So, they say, abolish all porn because the First Amendment does not take precedent over the Thirteenth, the abolition of involuntary servitude, or the Fourteenth which guarantees civil rights, or the Eighth which forbids cruel and unusual punishment.

To advocate pornography is not to ignore the crudities and cruelties of some porn against some women. But it is to ignore some crude thinking about gender. Each time we use the word "women" in this context we need to realize that it subsumes within it billions of particular female persons each with thousands of particular traits, likes and dislikes that differ according to time and place, mood and taste.

The very question: "Is pornography harmful to women?" is harmful to women because it ignores these individual differences. The question reduces all women to a class concept, and while elevating that class to "equality" actually oppresses individual women by the logic that forces them to be included *nolens volens* in that class.

Therefore, many feminists refuse to follow Dworkin and MacKinnon, finding them more oppressive than the porn they would ban. First, because sexual relations are relations and not *eo ipso* violations, force being only one form of that relation, not sex itself. Second, they psychopathologize all sex: whereas bondage, fisting or fellatio may be for some at times not a deprivation of liberty but a practice of joy. Third, banning porn closes an industry and forecloses a person's pursuit of happiness to follow a vocation as a professionally trained actress, strip artist, writer, photographer or prostitute. We did not close down the garment industry because of immigrant seamstresses in sweatshops or the dark satanic mills of Dickensian England because of laboring children. Protections were enacted, injustices corrected, conditions upgraded. And the industries themselves improved.

Fourth, Dworkin/MacKinnon have fundamentally distorted the male/female relation in porn. Men ogle and leer and spend *not* mainly because of patriarchal depravity and abusive power so rampant in the society. No, it is because men are entranced by the mystery revealed in porn, the naked Other revealed. They are, as Camille Paglia[14] says, in awe and under dominion of the feminine Goddess. Porn reveals Her power. The abolition of porn would suppress the Goddess and so, I conclude, against Dworkin/MacKinnon, that its prohibition is not in Her name. Indeed, Susan Griffin,[15] "the pornographic mind is the mind of our culture"—tho' not as you argue because of men's inflammations but because of Her infilitration.

Arguments back and forth—censor everything! censor nothing!—omit the principle I have been elaborating through these pages. Whatever the violence, whatever the cruel bond-

age or degradation that is displayed by porn, these images of
exploitation are all *images*. Pornography, as the suffix *graph*
explicitly states, belongs to an imaginal reality—theater and
show, inked lines on a paper, paint on canvas, reels of mi-
crothin film. All are such stuff as dreams are made on, phenomena of lustful imaginings. Their reality is beyond the law.
The actual literal humans who portray these imaginal scenes
have recourse to the same measures that protect the citizen
against injustice in any occupation or situation. Equal rights
under the law for all, regardless of profession. But the imaginings themselves are unavailable to censorship, unreeling their
shows in the dream and in the mind, day and night, as archetypal functions of the natural psyche.

So, if we accept Susan Griffin's dictum, "woman who *is* nature," (*op. cit.* p. 71) then the unceasing generation of pornographic images cannot be a male province or even a male perversion. As natural, they must be the gift of the woman who
is nature, the gift of the Goddess whom Griffin herself ac-
claims, in the shape of Aphrodite *porneia*.

IV. Priapos and Jesus, Pothos and Shopping

We have attended so carefully to Priapos in this essay because he is instrumental in most hardcore porn, either
as what is depicted or what aimed at. If there is a God
in the disease, as Jung says, the God is Priapos, and is it not
wiser to pay obeisance to the God than be obsessed by the disease? Porn aims to resurrect his erection. For the idea of divine resurrection needs to be recaptured from Christian usur-
pation and placed where today it actually occurs, the insurrection of the flesh, as St. Augustine called his libidinal desires,
the resurrection of the pagan powers who have been pressed
into the flesh. The first sign of their unease is pink madness.

Three reasons why the Gods return first via pink madness,
all noted by Freud: a) the sexual libido is at the top of the pile
of two-thousand years of repressed contents; b) it is a most
forcefully urgent instinct; c) and yet an instinct easily meta-
morphosed into devious vicissitudes. Pink madness invades

especially the commercial world, pornographying shampoo, Hawaiian islands, coffee beans and Velveeta cheese. Pink madness sells the skin of automobiles and the smooth hairless bodies attached to Nordic-trak machines. All these images we watch daily are varieties of soft-core porn. Romantically tinted, fuzzily sensuous, languidly arousing. However, the God or daimon here is less Hermaphroditos the freak or Priapos the prick, than their lovely brother, Eros. His is the inflammatory appeal, the otherworldly seduction, the constant courting of the soul, tempting psyche to swoon with desire—follow me, come fly with me, I will give you voluptuousness. You recall Eros and Psyche had a child (Aphrodite was her Granny), called *Voluptas*, voluptuousness, defined by the Oxford English Dictionary as "of, pertaining to, derived from, resting in or characterized by gratification of the senses, especially, in a refined or luxurious manner; marked by indulgence in sensuous pleasures." Precisely that is what the aura of consumerism offers: indulgence in sensuous pleasures.

Consumerism of course appeals to the psyche, because Psyche is always entranced by Eros. She can't help but shop, if the mall and the catalogue are where Aphrodite works her seductions and where the tale of Eros and Psyche plays itself out in our time. Wherever we are lured, the psyche is caught in that myth. And I want to defend this soft sex selling against the proponents of hardcore. They want crotch shots and organ grinding. No wrappings and trappings, no romance, no chiaroscuro, no fuzzy fadeouts.

The crucial criterion of hardcore content is direct concrete presence; nothing hidden, nothing absent. The reverse of this utter one-sided sexual literalism are the prudish censoring cover-ups, i.e., utter one-sided moral literalism.

This war between the two aspects of Priapos continues through the centuries, because there is always the fear that the demon may jump from the image, off the page, right into your lap, like that spark Malraux says which leaps from one person to another via an art object. The spark of arousal lurks; your erotic imagination could be stirred. Hence censorship: notorious are those by the Church of Michelangelo's

Last Judgment in the Sistine Chapel. Even the Bible has been found pornographic, censored and parts banned.

Flaubert wrote of these fig leaves and veils so acidly that I cannot resist an excerpt: Flaubert says he would have

> "given a fortune to know the name, age, address, profession and face of the gentleman who invented for the statues of the museum of Nantes those fig leaves made of tin that look like devices designed to discourage onanism. Casts of the *Apollo Belvedere*, the *Discus Thrower* and a flute player have been outfitted with these shameful metal drawers...affixed with screws to the members of these poor plaster figures now flaking away with pain...Amid the common stupidity which surrounds us, what a joy it is to find...at least one truly outstanding idiocy, one gigantic stupidity..."[12]

My point is that the covering *verifies* the priapic, transforms the athletic discus thrower, for instance, into a pornographic figure. Asinine stupidity (the object of Flaubert's scorn) belongs with Priapos. The statues move from nude art to naked pornography by virtue of the "shameful metal drawers." The importance of covering for the lustful imagination of uncovering suggests that Mapplethorpe's nude images are less pornic than the Apollo Belvedere who invites prurient peeking. Even Aphrodite stands at her bath, partly turned away, partly covered, yet nude and bare. Presence and absence both, for absence makes the heart grow fonder.

Nonetheless, as I said, advocates of hardcore want full exposure. For instance, Aretino, Renaissance journalist and hip porn-purveyor, writes:

> "What harm is there in seeing a man mounting a woman? Should beasts, then, be free-er than we are? We should wear *that thing* nature gave us for the preservation of the species on a chain around our necks or as a medal on our hats; for that is the fountain rivers of human beings come forth from...That thing made you...it created me, and I am better than bread. It produced the Bembos, the Molzas, the Varchis, the Ugolin Martellis...the Titians, and the Michelangelos, and after them the Popes, emperors, and kings. It

generated handsome boys and beautiful women with their
'holy of holies.' We should celebrate all this by establishing
special holy days and festivities in its honor rather than confining it in a small piece of cloth or silk. Men's hands might
be well hidden since they gamble money, swear oaths, practice usury, make obscene gestures, tear, pull, punch, wound
and kill."[17]

Aretino today would be among those who argue for more
genitals on TV and fewer handguns.

I fear that neither Flaubert nor Aretino grasp that the tin
fig-leaf or small piece of cloth belong essentially with the
priapic. Coverup is essential to priapic arousal. Soft core, because it invites fantasy beyond what is presented, fetishizes
even more strongly an arousing image.

This argument obliges us to re-read the most important of
all coverings in our culture, the naked Jesus of the Crucifix-
ion. Those veils, bits of fabric and artfully placed screen figures between us, the viewers, and his genitals are not simply
to be read as literal censorship of his literal sexuality, to ban
sex from the mind of his devotees.[18] These guises that hide
and yet indicate serve as a soft-core gesture on the part of a
very sophisticated church (whose rules consciously controlled
for centuries the image-making of religious objects). Suggestive, discreetly placed cover-ups fascinate the worshipers of
this most holy icon of an all but naked God, binding us to the
image erotically, passionately, arousedly, just by the very fold
of cloth, the branch, or limb, or leaf, or cupped hand, closing
off the literal and opening into the imaginable, the implied,
sparking the fervor of fantasy. The determining icon of our
culture's religious consciousness, because it is priapic in its
genital presence and absence together, is a soft-core emblem
par excellence. And I say this not as an insult.

For the soft brings in Eros as Plato says. So, I, Aphrodite
favor soft core. But do humans ever fully get the nature of
Eros? Do they realize that part of its nature descends from
that parent, Penia (need) who always wants, as told in the
Symposium tale by Socrates (one of my all time lovers). This
congenital unfulfillment re-appears as an inner figure within

Eros called *pothos*[19] or yearning, a longing for what is not here, hard, now, sure, known and red, but away, diffuse, rosy. Soft porn yearns toward the unattainable, suffusing commercial banalities with the promise of lascivious sweetness, like the girl on TV sucking her forbidden Fruzen Gladje.

The dominant theme in all soft porn is the transgressive temptation, beyond the limits of the actual and the usual, like the romance pulp fiction on a drug-store shelf. Soft porn offers sex transfigured to mystery, the sacralization of sex redeemed from secular conformity by Aphrodite *charis*, the grace and charm of the unknown as the new. It frees the heart's yearning for a "first time" *in illo tempore*, a mythical time untouched by earthly burdens, a new person in a new way in a new place, clasped breathless bodies in sacred space, all absences now present in a bleak room off a roaring highway.

So, I, Aphrodite, and my boys, banned from secular civilization, return into its heart core through the allure of consumerism that makes us want, desire, reach out (*orexis*, the Greek word for appetite, coming originally from stretching out, as of the fingers). And appetite has in it *petere*, to seek, to go for it, (petition as seeking, begging) and petulance, that feeling when you don't get what you beg for. Inside the shopping appetite and reaching fingers of consumerism is *ptero*, the wing of a bird; our stretching hand, a bird's wing. The human hand is phylogenetically homologous with the structure of a wing, so that the reach of desire is the wing of a bird. As archaic as the pterodactyl are the flying fingers of the yearning spirit ransacking the discount tables in your local K-Mart.

Quite simply: Aphrodite's pink madness runs the world *sub rosa* in the guise of the consumerist economy. Of course shopping and television viewing are the first and second leisure activities of the American people. By means of her seductions, she keeps the world running, out there shopping. Government enacts laws against drink, against smoking and promulgates a "no" against drugs. But who and how prohibit shopping? What—no more catalogues???

If truth be told, I, Aphrodite, *invented* soft core. It is how I catch a culture with a pink hope, a desire for wings. And it is far more effective than hardcore because it has the power of a symptom: it both denies and offers what the psyche wants. Soft porn is a compromise, as Freud (another of my sons?) said of all symptoms. It invites the soul's yearning for the beauty and magic of Eros, but only tantalizes with fantasies of a ghostly lover unknown, unseen, like my boy Amor in Psyche's night, present and absent both.

Remember: beyond the cooled habits of lust in marriage, *performed* lust[20] has but two choices, the neurotic or the psychopathic. Either the sentimental idealizations of a screen romance or the zipless fuck of strangers without past or future. Freud himself said that actual does not satisfy the sexual libido and Reich gave his life trying to get it "right" by literalizing cosmic *pothos* into orgone energy. Only *pothos* fulfills the soul's invisible complexities because *pothos* cannot happen. Like the alchemical conjunction it is a dream, a miracle in the glass vessel of imaginal reality.

As I see things, soft porn is not an idealization of sex, as the Freudian grey-beards (Anna, too) might say, and therefore a defense against hard reality. Rather it is the heavenly aspect given by me, this Goddess, directly or via one of my sons, reminding the soul that it must always serve in my temple, where it will always be susceptible to a wondrous lifting up from this world and reminiscent of another, platonic, romantic and rosy-fingered, filling this consumer world with the golden glow of Aphrodite Urania, that otherworldly radiance which was always the main purpose of my being and the main significance of my smile.

And so consumerism is far more effective, and more pleasing, than censorship, because it diverts rather than castrates desire. Do not the moralistic attacks on the hardcore porn industry serve, in fact, the retail trade? Business seems to recognize that were hardcore more prevalent, frankly lustful images could drive pink madness from the market. Then shoppers might escape the trap of the consumer conundrum as phrased by Eric Hoffer: "You never get enough of what you don't really want."

V. Curiosity as Courage

I would like to place what I am writing here within the field of psychological heroics as practiced by the founders of therapy—the psychoanalysts of Vienna and Zürich, the clinicians of Paris and Nancy, the asylum psychiatrists of Germany and England, those pioneers who were courageously curious about the vagaries of the human imagination and whose province was the unacceptable and unrelenting moods, lusts and obsessions that feed the roots of imagination in each citizen, incarcerated or in the streets.

Our work has always been in defense of the oppressed rather than adjustment to the oppressor. Therapy takes the side of the victim. But today it is hard to distinguish who is the victim and who is the oppressor. Are we victims of pornography or is pornography the victim? The lustful imagination is persecuted by puritanical Victorianism whose roots go deep into the fundaments of religious orthodoxy that does not allow the mind its nature and the dream its sexual pleasure, condemning the freakish and twisted to the public stocks of political correctness. This persecution so splits lust from images and images from lust that images lose their instinctual vitality and, worse, lust loses its imagination, finding substitute satisfaction in brute literal enactments. A vicious circle of literalism creates what it seeks to prevent, so that the censor may be more an underlying cause of sexual violence than that which is censored.

The seeds of this literalism were handed directly to Moses (*Exodus* 20) in a commandment against graven images. The Almighty warned Moses that any graven image—even of birds and fish—infringes His Omnipotence and must therefore be more abominable in a cosmic sense than such ordinary no-no's as lying, larceny, adultery and murder. Clearly any image at all is a grave threat to the monotheistic mind. Let us nevertheless remember that the edict says you must not fix in stone (graven means chiseled) any fantasy whatsoever, including, then, the fantasy prohibiting a graven image. This has always been recognized somehow by Jewish observers who regularly present the Commandments iconically and ironically as two engraved stone tablets. So, to take the commandment against idolatry on the mono-level of a prohibition only is itself a literalization of the very instruction not to literalize, therewith setting the commandment itself in stone, turning it into an immovable idol, perduring to this day in the stoneheads of fundamentalism.

But that's only half—the other half occurs in *Matthew* (5:28) where we are urged not to make any distinction between a lustful image in the mind and actual adultery in behavior. This was the passage that got Jimmy Carter in trouble. In a *Playboy* interview he admitted looking with desire. He courageously admitted to lustful images. For literalist readers of *Matthew*, Carter committed adultery for there is no fundamental difference for the orthodox between what one imagines and what one does.

May we not by now conclude that the basic issue of pornography becomes neither obscenity nor sexuality. It is literalism, the single-mindedness which reads images unimaginatively and is thereby threatened by them, and so is driven to control all images especially those that are overtly vital, i.e., endowed with sexual potency.

By referring to *Matthew* and orthodoxy, I am reminding us of Christianity's investment in the control of lustful images, a never-ceasing concern that did not begin with the present Pope's dogmatic obsessions. It begins centuries ago when Christianity itself took shape *vis á vis* Paganism, as Christians called the contemporary religions by which they were surrounded. The struggle over pornography is the struggle with Paganism. And the pagan Gods and Goddesses return, as the repressed always return, said Freud, through the most vulnerable place in Christian doctrine: its *lacunae* in regard to pleasure, the body, and the mythic imagination. Aphrodite, Priapos, Persephone, Pan, Eros, Dionysos, Zeus—especially these are the Gods returning. Pornography is where the pagan Gods have fallen and how they force themselves back into our minds.

Owing to their presence I cannot support any censorship at all. I am obliged to validate all porn on the basis of its importance for resurrecting the archetypal imagination. I want to encourage curiosity in it, or what is now condemned as "prurient interest." I stand against the Christian writers, such as Fenelon (1651-1715), who elevated curiosity to the first of sins, above even pride. Before we choose among the parts let us first accept the whole, otherwise differentiation becomes one more insidious suppression. As Thomas Jefferson said, "Whose foot is to be the measure to which ours are all to be cut or stretched?" The statutes against assault and involuntary servitude and which protect minors and those in dependent positions, sufficiently deal with the injustices wherever they occur in society, including the pornography industry. Pornography is not a worse case of the exploitation and abuse of children, of bodies, of women or of physical cruelties.

The war against pornography is only obliquely motivated by the pious defense of hapless children, the protection of exploited women and the safeguarding of decent family values. The war is that ancient one of iconoclasm against images, of the spirit's highmindedness against the soul's natural proclivities, of purity against pleasure, of sentimentalism against Saturn, of the rule of ideals against the facts of life, or in short, the highminded Olympian Gods against the powers of the field, the soil and the Underworld. Aphrodite combined both: *porne* and *urania*; as Priapos was a protector against bad luck and a fertile gardener as well as a frighteningly phallic grotesque.

The suppression of pornography begins with confusing the sexually graphic with the obscene, thereby lowering our private bellies into privy filth. This is the main mode of iconoclasm in our time and, by the psychological law of *pars pro toto* (a part represents the whole), pornographizes our nude bodies and degrades sexuality of any sort. This first obscene madness necessitates the secondary pink madness of consumerism. Also, this obscene madness creates the convention of shame, that interiorized censorship which inhibits serious rational community folk, like you and me, from talking about porn. It only can mean talking dirty.

Well, I want to talk dirty—to you—dirty politics. The political fight is about control of the responses of a human's body, or as Thomas Szasz says, control of the citizen's body by the state, otherwise known as slavery. Perhaps, pornography needs a lobby comparable with the National Rifle Association. For the constitutional right to bear arms that so exercises citizens today depends first on an enlivened and personally owned body reclaimed from state control, so that the citizen can bear those arms with civic responsibility rather than random resentful rage.

Pornography thus becomes as vital to our political present and future as other areas of bodily liberty; the rights of assembly and speech; to go unhampered to the polls; the abolition of bondage; abortion rights; the right to end one's bodily life; to ingest substances of one's own choosing; to be protected by law against physical assault, discrimination, exploitation and unjust punishment.

To these fundamental liberties I am adding the right to fantasize. Fantasy is innate to human beings, as irrepressible as our other instincts. As such it is more than a private luxury, more than a basic necessity. Fantasy is as well a collectively human responsibility, calling for the conscientious, courageous and joyful participation by the citizen in lustful imaginings. Pornographic fantasies require their place in the body politic as part of its instinctual vitality, else the psyche's life and the society's welfare is thwarted. If pornography, as we have defined it, finds no societal support and instead societal suppression, then the citizen and the nation decline into shamed, passive-aggressive victimization, tied by soft pink ribbons and whipped by the frenzies of consumerism.

Notes

1. For a superb chapter on Priapos, see R. Lopez-Pedraza, *Hermes and his Children*, Zürich: Spring, 1977.

2. Walter Burkert, *Ancient Mystery Cults*, Cambridge: Harvard UP, p. 105.

3. The Gnostic, Justin of Monoimos, considered Priapos and God the Father to have been one and the same. Cf. Geoffrey Grigson, *The Goddess of Love*, London: Constable, 1976, p. 81.

4. The best contemporary guide to discovering Aphrodite's effects in human life is Ginette Paris' *Pagan Meditations*, Dallas: Spring, 1986.

5. Cf. David L. Miller, "Christ, The Good Shepherd," in his *Christs*, New York: Seabury Press, 1981, pp. 3-52 for a superb analysis of The Shepherd figure.

6. One of the great gardeners of all time was Thomas Knight, younger brother of Richard Payne Knight, nick-named "Priapus Knight" (1750-1824) who honored this God with the first modern treatise (1786): *A Discouse on the Worship of Priapos*. The money earned by Richard supported Thomas's endeavors—a gift of Priapos's fertility? cf. Grigson, *op. cit.*, p. 80.

7. K. Kerenyi, *Zeus and Hera*, Princeton: Princeton UP, 1975, p. 99.

8. Thomas Wright, *The Worship of the Generative Powers* [1866], in *Sexual Symbolism: A History of Phallic Worship*, NewYork: Julian, 1957, p. 100.

9. Compare James Joyce, *A Portrait of the Artist as a Young Man* [1916], Harmondsworth: Penguin, 1976. p. 205: "The feelings excited by improper art are kinetic, desire or loathing...The arts which excite them, pornographic or didactic, are therefore improper arts."

10. Murray S. Davis, *SMUT—Erotic Reality/Obscene Ideology*, Chicago UP, 1983, p. 238.

11. Cf. *The Sex Panic: Women, Censorship and "Pornography*," NewYork: Nat'l Coalition Against Censorship (Conference report, May 1993), p. 12.

12. The legal issues and their history are thoughtfully discussed, and thoroughly documented in Edward de Grazia, *Girls Lean Back Everywhere: The Law of Obscenity and the Assault on Genius*, NewYork: Random House, 1992; D. A. Downs, *The New Politics of Pornography*, Chicago UP, 1989.

13. Stacey D'Erasmo, "Pornography Archives," *Lingua Franca*, June/July 1992, pp. 51-52.

14. Melanie Wells, "Woman as Goddess: Camille Paglia Tours Strip Clubs," *Penthouse*, October 1994, p. 58ff.

15. Susan Griffin, *Pornography and Silence: Culture's Revenge Against Nature*, NewYork: Harper & Row, 1981, p. 3.

16. From Gustave Flaubert's *Voyages*, Vol. I, p. 203.

17. Quoted from Pietro Aretino, *Lettere il primo e il secondo libro* in *I Modi, The Sixteen Pleasures—an Erotic Album of the Italian Renaissance*, ed. Lynne Lawner, Evanston Ill.: Northwestern UP, 1988, p. 9.

18. See the convincingly argued and carefully documented, sensational monograph by Leo Steinberg, *The Sexuality of Christ in Renaissance Art and in Modern Oblivion October 25*, Cambridge: MIT Press, 1983.

19. I have discussed *pothos* at some length in my *Loose Ends*, Dallas: Spring, 1975, pp. 49-62. On the relation between *pothos* and perversion, see Al Lingus, "Lust," in *Spring 51*, and Davis, SMUT, *op. cit.*, p. 238, who writes, "Sex, in short, is not so much a worldly as an other-worldly desire..."

20. See Al Lingus, "Lust," in *Spring 51*, and his subsequent book, *Abuses*, Berkeley: California UP, 1994.

EROTIC ANALYSIS AND THE SHAPE OF EROS

JOHN HAULE

Recently *The Boston Globe* ran a front-page article on sexual misconduct by psychiatrists beginning with an anecdote in which a certain Dr. Mathews struggles to define his feelings for a patient with whom he has been sexually involved for several weeks: "You're not my sister, wife, mother, another friend, daughter. Who are you? My special lover?" The unidentified journalist observes, "He might have tried the truth—victim."[1]

Evidently the writer of the article had not a clue to the psychiatrist's emotional befuddlement, for it was treated as a prime example of a male therapist's mendacious arrogance. Meanwhile the latter was unable to appreciate the damage he may have done. In emotionally charged matters of this kind, the opposing sides pass one another like two ships in the night, orienting themselves by entirely different sets of coordinates. The individuality of both parties is lost when we

John Haule is a Jungian analyst in Boston. He is the author of *Divine Madness: Archetypes of Romantic Love* (Shambhala, 1990). This article is an abbreviated version of the first chapter of a book on analysis, Eros, and sexuality.

speak in collective generalities. On one side the journalist speaks the language of what Jung calls "collective consciousness"—what I prefer to call the "persona field," for it conforms itself to what "everybody knows," formulates into codes, and brandishes as self-righteous slogans: "boundary violation," "power differential," "dual relationship," and "acting out." There is a great deal of truth in the persona field, despite the blindness of its nocturnal course. My conscientious colleague Peter Rutter has articulated its wisdom in *Sex in the Forbidden Zone*,[2] although the publisher's blurb on the cover of the paperback edition also points to its great flaw: "Provocative...says all the right things." There is much to be learned from Rutter's book about how sexual involvement by therapists is based upon the woundedness and unconsciousness of both parties. He intelligently spells out the bad faith strategies on both sides. But the book is oriented entirely by the coordinates of the persona field.

Dr. Mathews, benighted though he may be, pours over a different map and calculates the angles of different stars. From the perspective of what "everyone knows," he is a cynical manipulator, a pitiful neurotic, or both. He stammers out his sister-wife-mother reply to an unreported question, for he is by no means ignorant of the persona field. He feels the force of its opinions like a great surging river he has little hope of resisting, and therefore has protected his numinous and illicit affair in careful silence. Nevertheless he has not felt himself isolated in quirky idiosyncrasy. His naive stumbling prose "says all the right things" from the collective world of the archetypes where primal truths have stood unchallenged for millennia rather than decades. In the collective unconscious, where *his* ego has dissolved, his patient/lover embodies all of womankind and very likely goddesshood as well. On being accused of sexual predation, he is flabbergasted. How could his supremely true and worshipful love be so miscast?

The opposing parties live in complete and absolute worlds, wholly separate, speaking non-cognate languages. From his vantage atop Mt. Olympus, Dr. Mathews hears his accusers as though they are speaking of the habits of monkeys in the

Amazonian rain forest. The journalist listens to him as though he were describing life on Venus. Both Venus and the Amazon, however, belong to the full range of human life. Of his near-death experience, for example, Jung tells us he was so enthralled by the "garden of pomegranates" where he witnessed the wedding of the gods, that he could hardly bear to return "to the gray world with its boxes."[3] What is common sense for one, is gray boxes for another. Even those who have studied the language of their opponents—Jungian analysts, for instance—often seem unable to resist the mesmerizing pull to evaluate the transcendent realities of Venus in monkey terms or to throw out common sense with the empty cartons.

Rutter illustrates this in a reply to one of his critics in the recent issue of *Chiron*. Pamela Donleavy, an assistant district attorney in Philadelphia who had been an analysand in an erotically charged and successful analysis, chides Rutter for ignoring the collective unconscious. She describes the transformation of the sexual field she shared with her analyst through what she calls (citing Robert Stein) the Pan/Nymph archetype. Rutter replies: "To me the Pan/Nymph chase, as they identify it, is a culturally-bound mythic motif through which the psyche reflects back to consciousness its experience of actual rape and other sexual boundary violations that abound in our culture."[4] For Rutter archetypes are nothing but land mines in the persona field. He uses the word *myth* repeatedly in his book, but always to mean dangerous and deceptive untruth.

Individuation, as Jung repeatedly makes clear, involves hewing a course of personal integrity *between* the two collectivities, deeply cognizant of the realities of each but seduced by neither.[5] It is regrettable to think that individuation may not be relevant to the "forbidden zone." A Jungian analyst who writes about these matters while eschewing all mention of the archetypal field may be suspected of being in flight from Eros, as Donleavy reads Rutter. Again we are faced with the specter of ships passing in the night.

As a start toward a commonality of discourse, I offer some preliminary reflections on the phenomenology of the erotic as

we encounter it every day in the hope that they will be sufficiently fundamental to win the acceptance of both sides. To
some degree, whenever we speak of "the erotic," we refer to
Eros. But even the Greeks did not name the same psychic
force every time they invoked the god. In the earliest texts he
is the son of Chaos and represents the attractive force behind
friendships, marriages, and the creation of cities. Later he is
the son of Aphrodite and embodies lust. We, too, refer to a
broad spectrum of experience when we speak of Eros.

There's no Eros in this group. These words were spoken to me
by an experienced analyst who had recently moved to New
England. She meant to imply that, in comparison to her experience with other groups of analysts, our Boston meeting
lacked something. I pretty well knew what she meant. There
was a good deal of the "gray box world" in our meeting. We
displayed little joy in our fellowship, the hearty glow of comrades who have been tramping up mountains and down val-
leys all day long. There was something guarded and mistrust-
ful about us. We were reluctant to share ourselves. We
showed no enthusiasm for our common work or our separate
projects. We were "all business." There was no flow, no spill-
ing over, no emotional infection. We were polite, dour, and
contained. No wonder attendance was low. We were a dread-
ful group, lacking both strife and affection. Apathy reigned.

When Eros is spoken of this way, there is no suggestion of
sexual feelings. What is meant is a general interpersonal vitality. Without it, couples and groups are sluggish and dispir-
ited. If we say there is a lack of passion, we imply that our life
together as human beings is barely tolerable without it. In the
language of the archetypal field, *Eros* is what animates our
meetings and gives them soul. Even the persona field is aware
that encounters are sometimes lively and sometimes mori-
bund. We speak of interest, affect, and involvement. We mean
that we are engaged, moved, drawn in. In this sense, every
analysis and every psychotherapy looks to Eros, by whatever
name. But if we say *therapeutic relationships do not work unless
they are erotic*, we run the risk of being misunderstood. As
the son of Chaos, Eros brings confusion, and as the son of

Aphrodite lust. With our omnipresent wariness for being mistaken in such an emotionally charged dispute, we are careful about what we say.

A man who was seeing me for supervision introduced his problem with a new analysand by saying, *The moment she passed through the door, the room was charged with Eros.* Clearly he did not mean merely that he felt a fellowship with this woman or that he knew they would be able to converse with interest. He meant he felt Chaos threatening, and with unmistakable sexual overtones. Much to his relief, he found the sexual feelings diminished substantially in succeeding weeks. But Chaos continued to threaten. He found himself alternately pulled in by a boundless neediness and cast universes away by outbursts of rage. I thought of an analysand of mine tormented by a need to possess and worship me combined with a terror of intimacy which kept her locked so tightly in a shell I was unable to feel her violent emotions. I had immense compassion, but the channel that might have been empathy was cut off by the casing of her fear. Although she was gray and wrinkled, I saw her as a skinny, naked girl of four or five, crouching inside a glass cube, watching me warily out of the corner of her eye.

If Eros was in the room when I sat with that woman, it took a peculiar form. There was so little of fellowship I often thought I might as well be working with an alien that had learned my language. Yet I was bound. Although unable to return her feelings for me in kind, I could not accept an invitation to go out of town without first calculating what effect it would have on her. Her obsession had induced a peculiar reciprocity on my side. If it was Eros that brought us together, it was certainly not at all as lovers—perhaps as father/mother/god and alien waif. I found myself in a field of fragility, a clumsy lout in a storeroom of delicate glasswork, an inept divinity unused to worship.

I loved that woman, though it may seem peculiar to say I loved her erotically. I am even more reluctant, however, to use the other two expressions we have inherited from the Greeks to designate love. *Philia* denotes friendly affection,

and *agape* Christian charity. These terms suggest a calm cen-
teredness that denies the chaotic passion we ascribe to *eros*. I
felt myself drained, thrown into confusion, and on dangerous
ground. I could easily "say the wrong thing" and inflict even
more pain and turmoil upon her. Indeed I did so, all too often. My competence as an analyst was called into question,
even my competence as a human being to respond to a fellow
creature. The very ground of my existence was challenged by
this analysand, the assumptions on which I based my life, the
philosophy that underlay my teaching and writing. I felt passionately about these things. I was compelled to grapple with
them and to find a way to respond to this woman simply and
from my heart. In this we were surely similar, for her passion
battered and surged against the inside walls of her glass cage.
Her feelings, as she sometimes named them, were even sexual
in a naive, childish way. She fantasized marrying me as purely
and impossibly as my friend's four-year-old daughter had
done some twenty years earlier.

If we have trouble agreeing that *Eros* charged the interpersonal field between me and my severely inhibited analysand, it
may be the lack of symmetry that gives us pause. When we
consider the analysts' meeting that *had no Eros*, surely it was
symmetrical passions that we missed. Colleagues vitally engaged in their professions and their lives are expected to be
able to overflow with psychic energy and infect one another
with their kindred enthusiasm. But lack of symmetry does not
seem so much a problem when we consider my friend's
daughter. My adult affection and her childish emotionality
flowed and bonded us, as she showed me her crayon drawings
and somersaulted in and out of my lap while I talked with her
father of politics and social justice. That little girl and I felt
passionately about one another in a manner that went beyond
philia and *agape*. Our love was erotic, although innocent of
sexuality and lacking symmetry.

Symmetry, too, was evidently lacking between Dr. Mathews
and his patient/lover/victim mentioned in the *Globe* article.
The report implied she had sued him for sexual impropriety,
unassailable evidence that his feelings for her were not recip-

rocated in kind. Yet this asymmetry does not at all stand in our way of agreeing that their relationship was erotic in the usual sense of the word. We often speak of love relationships being out of balance, particularly when one party does not return the other's love. We have no trouble calling these one-sided bonds erotic. Consequently we must look for some other factor if we have difficulty agreeing that my relationship with my glass-caged analysand owed its power and fascination to Eros.

Possibly we hesitate on account of the unmistakable *inhibition* that characterized our sessions. Surely inhibitions played a crucial role in keeping Eros *out* of the meeting of analysts described above. Furthermore, the evidence for erotic energies in Dr. Mathews' dealings with his patient/lover/victim rests very heavily upon his *lack* of restraint, as was also true of the uninhibited playfulness between me and my friend's daughter. So there seem to be good reasons to build a case for the incompatibility of Eros and inhibition. But we are not consistent on this point. Presumably we would have no difficulty agreeing that Dr. Mathews should have inhibited his sexual response to his patient, regardless of how erotically he was drawn to her. And when my supervisee reported *the room was filled with Eros*, we are confident from his anxiety that he had been successful in inhibiting his response, although he feared he might lose his composure.

Clearly therefore, inhibition and erotic energies are not mutually exclusive. In fact we sometimes become alerted to the erotic nature of an interpersonal connection when inhibition emerges as a problem for us. We feel ourselves in danger of being overwhelmed by a need to express, ratify, and further the bonding impulse. Even in our private lives, we may very well be afraid of the Chaos this draw toward another may occasion in our orderly world. We hesitate and inhibit with the result that the impulse seems to gain in strength. In an analytic relationship there is no question that our commitments will conflict with the erotic impulse; and in most cases we direct our attention to how, why, when, and to what extent the analyst may be expected to inhibit his response. It is hard to avoid the conclusion that inhibitions—present or absent—are almost always a problem when Eros enters the space between us.

But with regard to my glass-caged analysand, we remark at the strength of *her* inhibitions. That is where the main problem seems to lie. We might be inclined to say that her passion remained locked inside of her and never overflowed to take possession of the interpersonal field. If so, was Eros barred from the analytic interaction? It would be hard to say so. For despite all its frustrations, her passion bound us to one another and awoke a different but equally vital set of emotions in me. This was so much the case that *our relationship itself became the primary issue between us*. Even though her inhibitions were overwhelmingly unconscious (in contrast to the predominantly conscious ones we just considered) and even though these inhibitions cut short her passion before it could flow out of her, they still determined our interaction and kept our attention on *us*.

Perhaps the most comprehensive thing we can say of Eros is that when he enters the room our *we-ness* takes center stage, the numinosity of our connection to one another enters our mutual consciousness. In this sense, surely, my work with the glass-caged woman was erotic. The same applies to Dr. Mathews and to my supervisee. In an attenuated way it also applies to the dull professional meeting we have considered. For insofar as we remained in our "gray boxes" that evening, we never experienced ourselves as a *we*. In summary, it can be said that our meetings must be sufficiently erotic to bring *us* to presence, to engage us, and to make our common work interesting enough to pursue. But at higher energies the erotic factor forces our *we-ness* to the fore and makes our relationship itself the central issue. In such situations we have no choice but to address our mutuality directly.

In the foregoing discussion we have discussed Eros entering the room as though unbidden. There are times, however, when we speak in another way. We might say, possibly of an analysand, that *he eroticizes all his relationships*. As far as I have been able to observe, it is primarily of *other individuals* that we say such things. This is "interpretation" talk, by which we mean the "eroticizer" finds himself in erotic relationships so frequently as to appear an exception to some unspecified norm. We grant that some individuals seem to be immune to his erotic influence. But we observe *we-ness* so frequently coming to presence in his encounters that we hold him personally responsible for this state of affairs. There must be an imbalance of some kind; for Eros, Son of Chaos, God of Lust, seems to enter every room when he passes through the door. *We-ness* really does obtrude chaotically again and again for him.

How does the alleged eroticizer himself experience these meetings? My exposure to such individuals leads me to conclude that generally—perhaps universally—they find themselves as much the recipients of erotic attention as do their partners. They do not voluntarily invoke Eros and may even be surprised and baffled by his frequent presence. For them as for us, Eros comes without being called, bringing the *we* inescapably to presence. But the very fact that we have found and labeled such a class of "eroticizers" implies something else essential about our view of Eros and the erotic. In claiming that some individuals, whether they know it or not, have a special capacity for generating erotic energies, we imply that Eros *is* called. Not consciously perhaps, but called nevertheless. We imply an unconscious will that calls even while we remain unaware of it.

Possibly it comforts us to think that when the Son of Chaos enters the field between a couple, he may have been called by one and not by the other. Perhaps it minimizes *our* responsibility that our unconscious will has only *welcomed* the erotic confusion into which we fall. Someone else has initiated it. Responsible for its origins or not, however, we find ourselves in a difficult situation that presses for decisive action. When we ask who did it and how did it get started, we may be searching for some sort of orientation in our confusion. But whatever answers we get for these questions, we are left facing the essential issue: what are we going to do about it?

As the answer to this question will always be the individual response of a particular analyst to a particular analysand met in an erotic field unique to that couple, it will not be possible to review all the possibilities. What can be done, however, is to provide a general frame for the question and its decisive response. We need a phenomenological description of the analytic field when Eros enters it so disruptively as to take us beyond the stage of "sufficient interest" to the point where our *we-ness* becomes a problem. We need to grasp the *structure of erotic interaction*. We shall begin by considering the nature of the erotic field as it may manifest in *any* human interaction. Thereafter we shall take up the specific peculiarities of the analytic situation.

Whenever Eros is felt as a disruptive force, our *we-ness* has come so forcibly to presence that our *I-ness*, our individual identity, is called into question. *I* and *you* as distinct entities are overshadowed by a numinous *we* that would subsume the qualities that define us as independent persons and dissolve us into a unity. It is the distinguishing characteristic of Eros that he lends to this *we* such a compelling, attractive force that we do not simply wonder if we can stand against it. We *want* to dissolve. Generally it seems to us that we have never wanted anything so vitally in all our lives. We would gladly shuck the confining limitations of our past and present self-image as a cruel delusion, now happily outgrown.

The *we*, however, does not simply fascinate us as a distant possibility. We find we are already part of it. Although dissolution lies before us as a seductive opportunity, we feel we are even now incomparably more than we were a moment ago. Enlargement, numinous *becoming* is already underway. Paradoxically, we find we have never been so much ourselves as we are at this instant. We are in the hands of a benevolent fate, witness to a glorious revelation, transformed at the root of our being. We stand on new ground, understanding profoundly and for the first time the unity of *all* beings. Our sense of *we-ness* is the window and door upon a new life. Our eyes are opened, the world becomes animate.

The *we* comes to presence, however, only through the unique and irreplaceable *you*. It may even seem to me that you constitute our *we* more essentially even than I. For I have been "just myself" all my life, but you seem to have brought our *we-ness* with you. It was unimaginable without you and distinctively *belongs* to you. Its every precinct is redolent of *your* unique personhood. You dominate the *we* so thoroughly that I may even forget my own participation and believe that it is in *you* that I wish to dissolve. It never occurs to me and cannot be the case that you are a mere occasion for my entering this *we*. You hold my fate as no other individual could ever do. For I have no fate more momentous and compelling than that which is brought to presence in the *we* which you and I comprise.

This is the work the Greeks ascribed to Eros, the Bringer of Union. He infects us to the core of our being, transforming us into a single pole of a dyad that yearns to trade its duality for a luminous oneness in which all meaning and vitality seem to dwell. But in the midst of this immense draw, a dissent rings out. Deep in our conservative and habitual sense of being our own unique selves, we rebel against this union. We view with horror all that we have known of ourselves being lost irreplaceably. We find ourselves on the brink of disaster, our balance deeply compromised, an instant away from plunging into the death of our individuality. All our instincts for self-preservation are mobilized and thrown into high gear. We steady ourselves against the rock of our remembered identity and prepare to flee. We shield ourselves with notions of having been deluded and blinded in our longing to dissolve. We rehearse a catalogue of our life-long beliefs and aspirations and hope they are strong enough to hold out against a demonic force that would destroy them. We step back from the precipice, and breathe deeply to calm our beating heart. But we do not turn tail; for the moment we lean away, our *we-ness* calls out to us with even greater urgency; and we prepare again to jump.

As we oscillate thus between the forward urge to dissolve and the panic to retreat, our anxiety becomes overwhelming.

This is the work of Eros, Son of Chaos. Temptations to terminate the tension abound. Among the most common forms are rage and lust.

When I react with rage to the intolerable anxiety our *we-ness* generates, I hold you responsible for the pain of my fragmentation. I hardly recognize myself as the victim of this devastating urge to dissolve and equally powerful need to flee. Your appearance has confronted me with such an insuperable inner division I fear I may never be whole and intact again. I convince myself that you are personally responsible for this state of affairs. In bringing about the loss of my coherent sense of being a self, which you alone have accomplished, I can hardly avoid the conclusion that you actually wish for my destruction. You embody all the evil forces of seduction, malice, and hatred that would bring me down, humiliate, and annihilate me. In self defense I believe I must either destroy you or erect an impenetrable wall between us. My rage is so murderous and frantic that it distorts and denies your unique personhood, replacing you with a distorted and demonic cipher that is not at all you but the projection of all my fears. In destroying you I destroy as well the *we* that emerges between us. I seek to banish Eros and return to my narrow and isolated sense of *I*, my illusory independence and self-sufficiency.

If rage radically denies erotic mutuality in an attempt to restore the *status quo ante*, lust would seem to be its polar opposite. For lust moves me to approach you as aggressively and one-sidedly as rage drives you away. But it seeks to terminate my anxiety just as resolutely. When I lust for you, I gaze upon you with eyes of desire, seeing in you all that I have failed to be myself. You are the apple of my eye. You are a revelation of numinous otherness, an embodiment of all I might become. I cannot fully exist without you. I am obsessed with the need to leap the distance between us, resolve the tension that separates us and drives me crazy with desire. I need you as I have never needed anyone or anything before in my life. If only you will give yourself to me, I will be able to possess both our *we-ness* and myself. I want to join you to myself and end the torment of my indecisive oscillation between the *me* and the *us.* I would avoid the dissolution of my identity in the seductive *we* by adding *you* onto myself as an object that enlarges but does not challenge my habitual sense of who *I* am. In so doing, I reduce your unique otherness and autonomy to a set of qualities that I may employ for my own purposes. Lust, therefore, denies the *you* while hoping to preserve the *we.* But it deludes itself in so doing, for there is no *we* without *you.* Eros, God of Lust, appears as a distortion of the Son of Chaos, a narrow and self-defeating ruler confined to the bad lands of his former domain.

The structure of erotic interaction, as it has been observed so far, makes it fairly clear that the call of Eros discernible in our *we-ness* can be heard and responded to only when the two of us can maintain both our own separate integrity and our participation in the unity that comes to presence between us. The urge to abort the tension between the *I* and the *we* may seem more than we can bear. But when I am able to bear this tension, I enable *you* to come to presence in your full and unique otherness. Instead of attaching myself to a single limited image of you—as in lust or rage—I allow you to be yourself in all your manifold otherness. I get to know the many facets of your being and how they express your center, the nucleus of your personhood. A process of revelation takes place, as I get to know you over time and enjoy your becoming. You do the same with respect to me. We reveal ourselves to one another; and as we do so, each of us comes to discover his and her own identity anew. In this development our *we-ness,* which we never leave, becomes a kind of lens for bringing one another and ourselves into focus. We influence one another and grow in the light of the *we* that challenges us and draws us after itself. Sexuality may be one of the many modes of our relating. But not having the one-sided and possessive character of lust, sexuality follows the call of Eros and resides in the *we-ness* that is brought to presence. If our individuality dissolves, as it surely will repeatedly, it restores itself naturally, changes, and grows.

This *structure of erotic interaction*[6] applies to all human relationships, including those conducted on the field of analysis or therapy. Considerations peculiar to analysis—such as the analyst's responsibility for maintaining boundaries of a particular kind—will emerge as refinements to this general picture. Specifically, there can hardly be any debate that an analyst is required by the nature of the therapeutic profession to pay special attention to the analysand's well-being and that this may involve a special kind of caution.

The Dr. Mathews, who stumbled through all the possible female relationship roles before settling on "my special lover" to describe his former patient, surely was insufficiently cautious. We may suspect him of fleeing a powerful *we*-centered pull through the tension-releasing mechanism of genital sexuality. We have no doubt that he enjoyed physical intimacies with his patient, and her raging reaction implies she felt he had gotten too close. If she had wanted their love-making to continue, she would not have sued him. Something had gone wrong between them.

There would appear to be two main possibilities—not at all mutually exclusive. If the numinous pull of the *we* had frightened her, the rage might have been generated by nothing Dr. Mathews actually did or said. Possibly she avoids all situations of intense intimacy because her sense of self is too precarious to risk obliteration in the promised unity of any *we* at all. Certainly Mathews should have known this or at least investigated the stability of her ego. If he acted in ignorance of or disregard for her uniquely personal set of fears, his behavior failed to respect her individuality. This is the second possibility. He failed to take sufficient care of her *you-ness*. Very likely he wished to possess her lustfully.

But his words do not sound like a man in the grips of Eros, God of Lust. True enough, he does speak possessively of *my* sister, wife, etc.; but he stands in awe before her. We may even detect a tone of adoration in his attitude. It reminds me very much of a passage from Teresa of Avila's *Conceptions of the Love of God*:

> But when this most wealthy Spouse desires to enrich and comfort the Bride still more, He draws her so closely to

Him that she is like one who swoons from excess of pleasure
and joy and seems suspended in those Divine arms and
drawn near to that sacred side and to those Divine breasts.
Sustained by that Divine milk with which her Spouse con-
tinually nourishes her and growing in grace so that she may
be enabled to receive His comforts, she can do nothing but
rejoice...With what to compare this [the soul] knows not,
save to the caress of a mother who so dearly loves her child
and feeds and caresses it.[7]

The gender and role confusions in this passage, where elements of father, husband, mother, lover, and savior are inextricably mixed, characterize many of the writings of the
Christian mystics—and, *mutatis mutandis*, the documents of
other religious traditions, as well.[8] Universally, the testimony
of religious mystics demonstrates how "full" the *we* may become. The fact that human lovers may slide over into mystical
language complements the tendency in mystics to draw upon
expressions of human sexuality. All of this adumbrates the
experience of the *we* when it comes to presence with archetypal numinosity.

To say that Dr. Mathews is lying to us and to himself when
he speaks of "sister, wife, mother, another friend, daughter,"
and "special lover," denies the phenomenological truth of his
experience. No wonder he feels we are prattling about the
habits of monkeys. He believes that the *we-ness* he has encountered in the presence of his patient/lover/victim has
transported both of them to the "garden of pomegranates"
where the "gray box" rules of the persona field are irrelevant.
Appeals to ethical codes and guidelines will always seem de-
structive and distorting to him. If we are going to communicate with him, we need a language that does justice to the realities of both the persona field and the archetypal garden.

A phenomenological description of the structure of erotic
interaction provides such a commonality of discourse. Here
we can grant Dr. Mathews the mystical dimensions of the *we*
as he has experienced it without relinquishing our right to
speak of the interpersonal nature of that *we*—of how it pre-
sumes both the *I* and the *you*, of how it arouses a nearly un-

bearable tension between the tendency to dissolve in sublime unity and the tendency to maintain our coherent and habitual sense of ourselves. We can speak of his patient's rage and inquire into its purposes—whether her ego was too weak to sustain *any* numinous *we* and whether he had assumed too much about her *you*. Perhaps he will come to see that the real and transcendental experience of *we-ness* that has meant so much to him deserves a cautious respect *on its own terms* and not simply because some gray ethics code says so.

Notes

1. "Psychiatrists and Sex Abuse," Boston *Globe*, Tuesday, October 4, 1994.
2. Rutter, P., *Sex in the Forbidden Zone* (Los Angeles: Tarcher, 1989).
3. Jung, C. G., *Memories, Dreams, Reflections* (New York: Pantheon, 1961), p. 295.
4. This issue of *Chiron* is still at the press as I write.
5. It is explicitly the theme of Jung's most basic and accessible work, *Two Essays in Analytical Psychology* (*CW* 7).
6. Described at length in Haule, J., *Divine Madness: Archetypes of Romantic Love* (Boulder, Colo.: Shambhala, 1990).
7. Cited in Pike, N., *Mystic Union: An Essay in the Phenomenology of Mysticism* (Ithaca: Cornell UP, 1992,) p. 75.
8. For example, the Sufis often speak of Allah as entangling the mystic in "her" dark tresses. The *sephiroth* of the Jewish Kaballah designate dimensions of father, mother, son and female lover within the Godhead. Hinduism names a plethora of divinities of varying genders and roles, all as personifications of the One, *nirguna brahaman*, which is beyond all specification.

APHRODITE GOES TO HAITI

JAY LIVERNOIS

*E*rzulie is the Haitian Aphrodite, the "voodoo goddess of love," so I would like to begin by giving a brief description of what "voodoo" is, although my real subject has more to do with Christianity and its constant whitening not only of Aphrodite but of sex itself.

Vaudun, as it is known in Haitian Creole, is a living polytheistic religion, originating and primarily practiced in Haiti, although, because of the Haitian "boat people" diaspora, *vaudun* ceremonies are now regularily performed in New York, Miami, Montreal, and other fortunate places. It is a syncretic religion made up of elements from West African "animism," Amerindian beliefs from the Caribbean basin, French Roman Catholicism and Masonic symbolism. *Vaudun* has a complete mythological pantheon whose gods and goddesses are called *loas* or *mystères*. Like Greek and Roman mythologies, there are deities for all the archetypes—for war, *Ogoun*; for the sea, *Agwe*; for death, *Ghede*; for fresh water, *Simbi*; the Haitian Hermes is called *Legba*, and so on.

Jay Livernois presented this paper at the 1993 Myth and Theatre Festival at Villeneuve lez Avignon, France. A lover of Haiti, he wrote the Foreword to Selden Rodman's and Carole Cleaver's *Spirits of the Night: the Vaudun Gods of Haiti* (Spring Publications, 1992).

times, instead of just providing knowledge to the *vaudunists* during a ceremony, a *loa* bestows power on someone present or cures an illness.

The actual act of possession has been best described by Maya Deren in the final chapter of her book, *Divine Horsemen: The Living Gods of Haiti*. Deren was a *vaudun* initiate and had the experience of at least once being possessed by *Erzulie* during a ceremony. She says the feeling of possession is like being in a "white darkness." Deren relates that when she first began to notice that she was being possessed, her left side became stiff and her left foot stuck to the ground. After noticing these sensations, she did not remember anything more. But for others who have experienced possession, it seems to occur all of a sudden, and they often feel as if they have just been whacked in the neck. Sometimes they faint and fall over seemingly knocked down by a strong wind. This possession and its oracle-like function is perhaps the most fascinating thing about *vaudun* from an archaic perspective, after of course, its mythology, which has provided a unique inspiration for the multicolored Haitian art and culture.

But why present the Caribbean Haitian goddess of love, *Erzulie*, at a festival in the south of France, in the ancient Roman territory of *Gallia Narbonensis*, in the Romantic province of Languedoc, the place of origin of the medieval courts of love, and the birthplace of the dark love of de Sade? Certainly not because she adds a multi-cultural aspect to this conference, or because Haiti and its mythology are exotic and primitive, and I want to add some sophistication to my merely being an American descended from English religious fanatics (Puritans) and French-Canadian outlaws. It is of course appropriate to bring *Erzulie* here because Haiti is, overtly, a francophone country, and this is France, and because André Breton, Pierre Mabille, and André Malraux, those high priests of modernism, "discovered" Haitian art and culture, and because their modernist visions were so informed by "African" primitivism.

But the real reason I want to talk about *Erzulie* here stems from the controversies that arose and almost drowned the last

"Myth and Theatre Festival" at Villeneuve lez Avignon in 1991. These controversies were centered on the different interpretations of the ancient world. I do not have a problem with differing interpretations and fantasies of what classical culture was like per se, whether they are from Marxist sociologists, Freudian art historians, French semioticians, or feminists reading Robert Graves' *The White Goddess* for the first time. But when these interpretations exclude other fictions, for political and (usually unconscious) religious reasons, a fanatical monotheism breaks out, as we saw here in 1991. The intellectual atmosphere at the last festival felt close to what I imagine has produced the situation in Bosnia and has led to Europe's strange impotence in the face of Serbian and Croatian Christians killing masses of Bosnian Moslems. At this point it is especially good to remember that there is a continual and relentless persecution (including the killing) of *vaudunists* in Haiti by Christians, often new fundamentalists, whose psychological intolerence of polytheism insists on destroying that pagan culture.

Ironically many people at these "Myth and Theater" conferences run around believing they are "born again pagans" or are intellectual or psychological polytheists, or they think they can literally identify with a goddess (usually expressed as *the* goddess within) or can now express their pagan "wild man," and they feel that they are spiritually part of a "New Age." Of course religiously, they cannot be anything more than apostates or syncretists given the Christian culture that they are born into and the pervasiveness of that culture. We do not live in a polytheistic world or culture, no matter how much we would like to think so, and we clearly have a difficult time imagining what European culture and religion was like two thousand years ago when polytheism was actually still alive. Consciously or unconsciously we remain monotheists because of the larger cultural context we find ourselves in. Even archetypal psychology, the most intelligently pagan of modern psychologies, comes out of a Jungian psychology heavily influenced if not unconsciously dominated by Protestant theology. Archetypal psychology itself admits to being

Jewish and Christian, besides pagan, but it really has little choice in the matter.

This Christian monotheism is not just in our heads, it is in our bodies. This fact became all too clear to me when I saw the restored ancient bronze statues of Riace displayed in Florence in the Spring of 1981. The now famous bronze bodies of the two male warriors are beautiful and striking, although not perfect or idealized. They contrasted dramatically, however, with the bodies of the people in the museum audience who were looking at the statues. The people had terrible posture with hunched shoulders, curved backs and no musculature. There were also many people who were grossly fat or paunchy with apparently no life, no lust in them. The crowd seemed like a collection of physical grotesques. The amazing thing was that this bunch of people was made up almost entirely of Florentine Italians—no American or German or English tourists (in case there are any Italians reading this who want to explain away this observation in the usual manner), and I was seeing this in Italy, the land of *la bella figura*, and in Florence, the city of the Renaissance. I asked the Italian I was with what had happened to the people of Italy in the last two thousand years to bring about such a shocking difference between the gorgeous statues before me and the ugly crowd. She unhesitatingly replied that Christianity had tragically broken the backs and bodies of the Italian people over the last two thousand years.

There is of course another place besides our heads and bodies where this Christian monotheism thrives, and this is in our souls. When we imagine the ancient polytheistic world of our ancestors, we always imagine it as a world of white marble classicism. Our fantasies have been formed by art museums full of age-bleached artifacts like the Elgin marbles or the Venus de Milo; or by Hollywood "sandal flicks" which always end with the hope of Christianity looming on the screen to save us from Roman slavery and orgy rape; or by the bloodless pedantry of classicists who in our schools read mythology as a primitive superstition and do not really believe in the power of their own material.

Ancient statues were of course not just white marble but
were painted with bright colors, adorned with gold, silver and
gems. They often had human hair, were clothed as well as naked and had magical talismans either fixed to them, hung on
them or inserted inside secret caches. Worshippers sometimes
even had sex with the statues, especially with statues of Aphrodite and with certain phallocentric gods like the Roman
bedroom deity Mutunus Tutunus. Blood and/or vegetal sacrifices were made to all of them, and in such quantities that
when it was warm, ancient temples would become covered
with flies; the smell of the temples in the summer must have
been unreal. I mention this only to point out how far we are
from a living sense of polytheism, and how our museum-based
imagining of it, because of Christianity, has so little to do
with what probably went on in the ancient world.

Haiti is thus enormously important and enriching to the
over-all culture of the world today. *Erzulie* and the other gods
and goddesses of that island make up a living polytheistic culture, though for how much longer cannot be said given the
present assault on *vaudun* by Christian fanatics. In Haiti we
can see how a polytheism works, and by studying its practice,
instead of smashing it, perhaps even get a better sense of how
the ancient world worked. From Haiti, we may even get a
better insight into the goddess-archetype of love as she works
through us.

At this point I would like to introduce—as a further challenge to you, and to show you how stuck we all still are on
these subjects—an account of a *vaudun* ceremony from a book,
Voodoo Fire in Haiti, written by Richard Loederer, a German,
in 1935. His whole sense of what he sees is informed by European monotheistic culture (which is still basically ours today)
that demonizes anything other than a single, transcendent
conception of God. I would like to point out particularily the
demonic yet seductive atmosphere of death and eros as described by the author. Loederer writes:

> As we rode through the night the drums were beating
> again—but with a new rhythm that I had never heard be-

fore. I was keyed up to a pitch of perspiring excitement, fearing what was to come and yet unwilling to turn back. We were about to participate in a monstrous performance, an orgy which not one white man in a million has ever seen. Tonight was a Voodoo Fire, and *we* were to be present.

I shivered as I rode along. I was horribly afraid; afraid of the night, afraid of the menacing drums, and above all, afraid of seeing *too much*.

The path climbed upward amongst the jagged hills. Below us lay the town and, far off, the sea, glittering in the moonlight. It was a warm night, yet the pale rays of the moon cast a chill aura of malignant evil over the scene. We rode through a cemetery where the whitewashed tombstones flitted past like serried ranks of ghosts, then the dark shape of trees rose up again on either side, stretching their gnarled branches in our way.

And all the while the hollow booming of the drums rang in our ears; now nearer, now further off, rising and falling in subtle cadences... The drums were calling, they drugged the will until all resistance died. I realized with impotent horror that it was impossible to turn back; the power of the drums was too great.

Suddenly we emerged into a wide clearing. In the middle was a huge fire and round it were at least two hundred negroes and negresses...

To the left of the fire a row of stakes had been driven into the ground. Fixed horizontally across them at the height of a man's head were crossbars from which depended five long conical drums. A gigantic naked negro stood in front of each, working like a fiend. Two of the men used short wooden sticks but the other three evoked a peculiar rhythm by gliding their finers and palms over the tightly stretched goatskins. The drums responded to the efforts of these sweating blacks with a shattering resonance of sound.

Suddenly a negress wearing a white chemise and a scarlet sash stood up. It was the Mamaloi...

Backwards and forwards danced the Mamaloi. In and out between the rows of squatting figures. Her eyes were fixed in a rigid sightless stare and the sweat poured down her body. Saliva ran from her mouth, trickling down her neck and between her breasts. She approached the fire...

A violent fit of trembling shook the woman. It was as if a demon lover had taken possession of her and were exploring her limbs to their very extremities. Someone handed her a black cock which she raised high above her head. The scene was diabolical. There stood the naked negress, her sweat-streaked body glistening in the ruddy firelight, and at arm's length she held a terrified black cock, the very symbol of Satan, squawking and flapping its wings, while the feathers flew in all directions. An awful sickness gripped me. I felt as if I were looking into the very depths of evil. The thunder of the drums grew to an avalanche of deafening reverberations.

Slowly the body of the Mamaloi relaxed from its rigid posture. She began to turn; faster—faster—faster. Like a madman she spun round on her toes. She swung the cock now only by its legs and as it flew through the air in dizzy circles it spread its wings wide in the last convulsions of death. As though carried through the air by the beating pinions the negress whirled forwards in frantic ecstasy. The drums rose to their shattering finale, the woman stopped motionless, and then—a miracle—the dying cock twisted its neck convulsively and crowed—crowed loud and raucous into the surrounding night. It was the final touch of horror. (265-71)

From this account it sounds like Loederer witnessed a ceremony to either *Erzulie* or to *Damballah*, the Haitian ambisexual fertility god. Unfortunately the version is so sensationalized and lacking in important details, it is hard to tell exactly what he saw—that is, if Loederer actually went to a ceremony at all. It is possible he just made the account up. In any event what we clearly have here is the combination of terror and erotic fascination that the darkness in polytheism holds for Christian eyes; like Mr. Kurtz in Joseph Conrad's *Heart of Darkness*, going up the Congo with his trading boat full of Christian culture, only to die in what is for him its erotic "heart of darkness," and crying out at the end of his long, stange trip, "The horror, the horror."

So often when we talk or write about Aphrodite, we see her monotheistically, filled with the white marble and pious rhetoric of wholeness and union. I see this as a clear signal that we are profoundly misreading Aphrodite. Look at what a one-sided monotheistic interpretation she gets, for example, in a book many people love, *The Myth of the Goddess* by Anne Baring and Jules Cashford:

> By imagining Aphrodite at the very beginning of the process of creation when Heaven and Earth are parted—as the Orphic myth does with Eros—love is drawn in the greater perspective of humanity's longing for reunion with the whole. Aphrodite is no longer the one Great Mother Goddess who is the origin of all things, but, as daughter of the sea, she is the child of the beginning. Consequently, she is the figure who, in the likeness of the original goddess, brings back together the separate forms of her creation. In this sense Aphrodite is 'born' when people joyfully remember, as a distinct and sacred reality, the bonds that exist between human beings and animals and, indeed, the whole of nature. The myth proposes that this happens through love. Union is then reunion, for love that begets life resounds with the mystery of life itself. (353)

Almost twenty years earlier the great Jungian classicist, Karl Kerenyi, expressed a similar monotheistic vision of Aphrodite in his book on the *Goddesses of Sun and Moon*. He wrote:

> The images of Anadyomene rising up out of the depths of the sea, is the transparent purity of complete union become visible. Through Aphrodite the whole world becomes pellucid and thus so brilliant and smiling, because in her the opposites are dissolved into unity, and this unity reveals to every living being the possibility of the same unproblematic—using the current adjective, though said in a more Greek way it would be calm-sealike—situation. (58)

The problem with both of these visions of Aphrodite is that there is no dark side or shadow to the goddess. In a living polytheistic system, a godddess or god holds both good and bad attributes at the same time. In a monotheistic system, a goddess or god does not carry any evil or darkness, it is split off. Christ has no shadow, at least for Christians, but the Devil then comes into existence.

Kerenyi says of Aphrodite, "Under the sign of Aphrodite we are not dealing with something heavy and darkly earthy, with an unconscious dissolution into a state of fusion, but rather with something bright and lucid" (58). Baring and Cashford also see no shadow to Aphrodite. They write, "As an image arising in the human heart, Aphrodite comes alive when the animal nature of humanity is experienced as divine. She is there whenever life sparkles with beauty and joy" (351).

The problem with all this sweetness and light is that polytheistically goddesses and gods not only carry shadow, but we often contact them—and they often contact us—most vitally through shadow. It is as daimon, demon, symptom, madness, disease—and what the Apostle to the pagans, St. Paul, so contemptuously called *porneia*—that the *pagan* goddesses and gods press themselves on us, move in, by, and through our souls. Without shadow, demons and *porneia* (the dark erotic images), there are really no goddesses or gods moving in the soul, just white marble concepts that we manipulate like medieval scholastics or modern scientists.

One only has to look at the classical myths of Aphrodite to see this shadow. Yet if one is seduced into a vision of Aphrodite as an example of wholeness and union, it disappears.

What is Aphrodite's shadow? Well to begin with, Aphrodite is born out of the violent act of the castration of her father, Kronos, which is euphemistically and strangely described as a "harvest"(!, 353) by Baring and Cashford. She also has the power to make men impotent which can be seen as a non-surgical form of castration. This is clearly illustrated in the *Homeric Hymns* where a disguised Aphrodite seduces Anchises. After they make love, she reveals "her goddess within," and Anchises begs Aphrodite not to make him forever impotent.

> ...and begging her, he spoke these words: "Right then when I first saw you with my eyes, goddess, I knew you were divine. But you didn't speak honestly to me. Now at your

knees I implore you, in the name of Zeus who carries the
aegis, don't permit me to live impotent among men from
now on. Pity me. For a man who sleeps with immortal goddesses loses his potency."

("The Homeric Hymn to Aphrodite (I)"
trans. Charles Boer)

More than just a castrator in this myth, Aphrodite has lied to
and deceived Anchises to get him to fuck her and make her
pregnant (with Aeneas). She then proceeds to destroy his life,
the life of his family, and his country by bringing about the
Trojan War. Talk about fatal attraction!

Contrary to the willful blindness of contemporary goddess
mythographers, Aphrodite even had an underworld connection in the ancient world which gave further depth to "the
Golden One." At Delphi an *Aphrodite of the graves* was wor-
shipped. Prostitutes who specialized in graveyard locales,
nicknamed "butterflies" in the ancient world, were especially
fond of this cult at Delphi.

In addition, some of Aphrodite's surviving epithets hint at
the shadow we seem no longer able to see. She was known as
Melaina and *Melainis*, "the black one," and *Skotia*, "the dark
one." She was also called *Androphonos*, "Killer of Men,"
Anosia, "the Unholy," *Tymborychos*, "the Gravedigger" and
Epitymbidia, "she upon the graves." These names point to
Love's orgasmic and tortuous connection with Death and the
dead. What can be darker or more chthonic than this?

Here is where *Erzulie* and *vaudun* are so helpful. The goddesses and gods of Haiti have not lost their dark sides like our
classical ones, because polytheism is still alive there. As a result *Erzulie* is not only the Haitian goddess of love, but the
goddess of murderous jealousy as well, of sex for pleasure with
absolutely no connection to fertility, and the goddess of a
kind of wasteful luxury (horrific when seen from a Protestant
perspective but understandable in pagan and Catholic Haiti).
Erzulie is also portrayed as a bimbo, a slut and a gold-digger.
She whines and complains that she is not waited on enough,
and that she is not loved enough. *Erzulie* cries, can go into

rages and be thrown into despair. She can be promiscuous yet demand total faithfulness from her multiple lovers. She can never make up her mind as to what to wear or eat or drink. In short, *Erzulie* can be, and is, wonderfully irrational, neurotic and impossible, just like so much of the experience of love.

For Haitians, as the goddess of love, she is not just "beauty and joy" or "union and reunion." That would be ridiculously too simple. For in *vaudun*, *Erzulie*, like all the Haitian *loas*, carries the demonic. She is as differentiated as love is itself, with all of its beauty, ugliness, terror and shadow.

In v*audun*, there is not just one manifestation of *Erzulie*, just one goddess of love, as our monotheistic imaginations would have there be only one Aphrodite today. For Haitians, the fragmentation, differentiation, and sometimes even con-flation of a goddess or god echoes their vitality. So in *vaudun* there is *Erzulie Freda Dahomey*, *Maitresse*, *Gran Erzulie* (her grandmotherly version), *Erzulie Dantor*, *Erzulie Ze-rouge* (red-eyed and jealous), *Erzulie Toro* (bullish and butch-like), *Erzulie Mapian* (louse-like and biting), *Erzulie La Belle Venus*, *Erzulie Severine Belle-Femme* (her My Fair Lady incarnation), *Erzulie Dos-bas* (meaning lower back, an *Erzulie* "always on her back"), *La Sirene Erzulie*, and *La Baleine Erzulie* (the whale-like *Erzulie* "for those who like their lovers big").

Here in La Chartreuse I present to you these dark and different images of *Erzulie* from the living polytheistic tradition of Haiti not for polemic or analysis—please—but as a deeper way of seeing our own classical Aphrodite. I do not want to bury Aphrodite in images of *Erzulie* but through them to praise her, dark side and all.

Works Cited

Baring, Anne and Jules Cashford. *The Myth of the Goddess: Evolution of an Image*. New York: Viking, 1991.

Boer, Charles, trans. *The Homeric Hymns*. 2nd ed. Dallas: Spring Publications, 1989.

Deren, Maya. *Divine Horsemen: The Living Gods of Haiti.* New York: Thames & Hudson, 1953.

Kerényi, Karl. *Goddesses of Sun and Moon.* Trans. Murray Stein. Dallas: Spring Publications, 1979.

Loederer, Richard A. *Voodoo Fire in Haiti.* New York: Doubleday & Co., 1936.

Rigaud, Milo. *Secrets of Voodoo.* Trans. Robert B. Cross. San Francisco: City Lights Books, 1969, rpt. 1985.

Rodman, Selden and Carole Cleaver. *Spritits of the Night: The Vaudun Gods of Haiti.* 2nd ed. Dallas: Spring Publications, 1994.

PSYCHOLOGY AS FATHER
RELATION AND FEMINISM
AS ACTING OUT

ALAN HAMILTON

Hounds of madness, fly to the mountain, fly
Where Cadmus' daughters are dancing in ecstasy!
Madden them like a frenzied herd stampeding
Against the madman hiding in woman's clothes
To spy on the Maenads' rapture!
—Euripides, *The Bacchae*

The image of Pentheus disguised as a woman and led by his curiosity to hide in a tree in order to spy on the Maenads' ecstatic celebration of Dionysus, is, I propose, an image of our detached psychological point of view and perhaps a harbinger of the dangers inherent in such a perspective. "We live fundamentally in a super-terrestrial world of ideas cocooned in irreality," states Wolfgang Giegerich. "And psychology does its best to help instill and envelop human existence in this bubble" (1993). The irreality

Alan Hamilton lives in Lamy, New Mexico, and is working on a Ph.D. in Clinical Psychology at Pacifica Graduate Institute.

to which Giegerich refers is the perspective of Pentheus, the point of view of the non-participating observer in relation to the actuality of experience. This irreality of ideation and conceptualization is, in Andrew Samuels words, the father relation:

> The father relation, which is in its essence cultural and psychological, is the paradigm for our capacity to regard any relationship from a psychological point of view (1989, p. 72).

The dominant nature of our patriarchal culture is experienced as the need to objectify and conceptualize the world in terms of relationships between persons and things. It is a bias of the father relation, however, that finds meaning solely within relationships while forgetting, and thus subjugating the tings themselves from which relationships are derived. In further exploring Samuels' notion of the father relation as psychological perspective, it will be determined that psychology is losing a fundamental link to reality (Giegerich, 1993). In our cultural determination towards omnipotence and the control over our destiny, we have denied, or perhaps forgotten, that all ideas, conceptions and images are inextricably linked to the world body. Culturally the feminine *relation* to the actual world has been increasingly ignored; it has been suppressed, denied and sublimated in man's quest for meaning derived exclusively from a perspective of distance. The feminine relation refers to a symbiotic and biological connectedness that a woman experiences with her child; it is biologically substantiated and primary rather than conceptual and relational (Samuels, 1989). It is my contention that all ideas and conceptions, all epistemology, are consummated and substantiated within our mortality, because it is mortality that remains the inescapable symbiotic and biological link to the world/body, the feminine. Our culture, along with its psychologies, must somehow reorient itself to the feminine lest we, like Pentheus, become an unwitting sacrifice.

In order to begin, let me roughly sketch Samuels' notion of father as a "created relationship." Samuels' argument begins with the distinction between the concepts of father and mother that are cultural derivatives of gender, which has its basis in biology. "Gender is the psychological and cultural analogue of biological sex; this implies a foregrounding of the cultural dimension" (1989, p. 70). It cannot be disputed that there is a difference between men and women anatomically or biologically. But the main difference lies in the biological fact that women can give birth and men can not. Consequently, the relation of infant and woman is primal and direct and "the relationship of father and child may be seen as arising out of two other relationships: the pair relationship between man and woman, and the primal relationship between woman and infant" (Samuels, 1989, p. 70). Because of the lack of the primal experience of birth, the "relation called father" is always cultural and psychological in essence.

To the extent that father is a created relationship, so, too, is the hierarchical and patriarchal cultural organization within our society. Samuels writes:

> Paradoxically, that the relationship called 'father' is a *created relationship* gives to it immense psychological and cultural significance...The created relationship called 'father' becomes the germ for an entire system of cultural organization based on kinship. For kinship is not 'natural', and certainly not universal in its shape or pattern (1989, p. 71).

Kinship is another term for a relationship that is not known unless it is declared. For Samuels, the father relation and all of its corresponding cultural manifestations, including psychology, are conceptual and abstract because they lack biological or "natural" grounding. The predominantly patriarchal culture, being created out of a lack of natural or biological limitations, surrounds itself in the delusion of autonomy to the extent that even the natural or biological relationship of woman and infant are perceived as the kinship relation of mother and child (Samuels). Because of the cultural predominance of the father relation and its tendency to construct and declare relationships, the collective notions that we have developed of the feminine are unnaturally correlated to women. Consequently, the cultural attributes of gender (masculine and feminine) and biologically determined sex (male and female) have become synonymous with each other. Samuels re-establishes the distinction between biological sex and the cultural phenomena of gender:

> Sex (male and female) refers to anatomy and the biological substrate to behavior, to the extent that there is one. Gender (masculine and feminine) is a cultural or psychological term, arising in part from observations and identifications within the family, hence relative and flexible, and capable of sustaining change (1989, p. 95).

The existence of the feminine, and its more authentic relationship with the world, exists to some degree in both sexes. When filtered through the cultural perspective of the father, however, the feminine is not only equated with women but more specifically with mother. When the nature of the feminine is approached by means of the father "or the *idea* or assumption that relations [are] cultural and psychological," the result is towards the regressive tendency of "gender certainty" in which woman is equated with mother and man equated with father (Samuels 1989, p. 71). It is a bias of the father relation that regards all relationships, and the meaning derived from them, as primarily psychological. Samuels contends that the strength of this perspective, evident in the patriarchal dominance within Western culture, arises out of the inherent vulnerability of the declared relationship between father and child:

> *The biological weakness of the father relation gives it its psychological strength.* For the father-child relation has to be *declared.* Indeed, whole chunks of patriarchal culture rest on this particular aspect of male vulnerability. We don't know the father is the father until we can apply the psychological idea and image of father. An image produces a relationship, it's pure psychology and tremendously difficult to handle (1989, p. 72).

Samuels' argument works to the conclusion that "the only thing archetypal about the father archetype is that there is nothing archetypal about the father" (January 1993). Perhaps an archetypal relation is fundamentally the same as the feminine relation, in that it is direct, essential and experiential rather than mitigated or conceptualized. Because psychology is based upon the father relation, about which nothing is archetypal, it follows that the only thing archetypal about psychology (even archetypal psychology) is that there is nothing archetypal about psychology.

This statement, and Samuels' statement from which it has been derived, need to be looked at closely, for there is a bit of the trickster within it. I do not interpret Samuels to mean that there is nothing archetypal about the father, but rather that *nothing* is specifically what is archetypal to the father and to psychology.   Although it is rather perplexing, let us consider more closely the "nothing archetype." The father relation, and the psychology which arises out of it, exist as a relationship between things and not within a symbiosis of the things themselves. Like the father, psychology is relational. It defines itself in terms of relationships between things, but is nothing in and of itself. This is another way of saying that psychology is metaphor; it connects and makes relationships to things that are normally or naturally unrelated.

Paradoxically, I believe that there is an image of the nothing archetype in the god of relationship and connection, the lord of the roads, the trickster and thief, Hermes. It is not surprising that many religious images that represent Hermes (*herms*) are rectangular pillars with a head and an erect phallus. It is the phallic aspect of Hermes that creates the possibility of imagination by defining the boundaries of the psychic space. Rafael Lopez Pedraza explains that "the first view of Hermes offered by our classical Greek scholars is as a 'stone heap.' The stone heaps were placed along the roads to mark them; they also marked the boundaries between villages, cities and regions, landmarks fixing the boundaries and frontiers" (1989 p. 14).

Hermes phallic work is towards relationship. His nature is divisive in that space must be made between things before the connection of relatedness can be made. As God of the roads he is dividing the territories to which he ultimately makes meaningful connections. He "marks our psychological roads and boundaries; he marks the borderlines of our psychological frontiers and marks the territory where, in our psyche, the foreign, the alien, begins" (Pedraza, 1989, p. 14). It is this phallic division that creates a new dimension of space between things; a nothingness that contains the possibility of relationship and meaning. Hermes' phallic divisiveness manifests the father relation. Hermes is the "patrix" of metaphor, piles of stones declaring new relationships within the unlimited frontier of the imagination.

The constructed nature of the father relation is the space, or absence, that exists within the declared separation from the biological actuality of the feminine, which in turn contains the possibility of metaphoric connectedness. The sort of meaning found in metaphor, imagination, conceptualization, or any sort of hermeneutics, is what I will refer to as phallic meaning. Phallic meaning is *understanding*. The word "understanding" implies a separation from the object in question. To stand under, or to see something from beneath is to be removed from the thing itself so that perspective is possible; a perspective from which relationships to other objects can be made. This phallic meaning created by perspective is the father relation. The overwhelming bias towards this perspective can be recognized in the word *confusion*, which is taken to be antithetical to understanding. To be fused with something is to be in a symbiotic relationship with it, merged and married to it. This is the feminine relation where distinction, separation and perspective are secondary to meaning that is essential and experiential. Yet, because we are culturally predisposed to understanding, confusion becomes the shadow or negative aspect of human nature that not only threatens our understanding, but also gives it the material to which its phallic enterprises are justified. Our aversion to confusion is in part the basis of the cultural repression of the feminine, the symbiotic relationship that we have with our bodies and the world, our sexuality and mortality.

In the past several decades we have seen an increasing need to rediscover and honor the feminine nature of ourselves and our culture. Jung's work on the anima, the feminine aspect of the soul, began a tradition of looking beyond the patriarchal mechanisms of scientific empiricism, towards a psychology more inclusive of the feminine soul, or psyche. But even the many branches of Jungian psychology that have worked to give a place to the feminine within its psychology have further contributed to her repression because of the insistence that she be experienced referentially or phallicly. In trying to approach the psyche with a psychology that is fundamentally derived from the kinship model of the father relation, we are allowing the psyche to exist primarily in terms of the perspective of the father.

Over the past several decades much work has been done to reacquaint ourselves with the dark, fecund and mysterious aspects of the feminine. Archetypal psychology in particular has explored many of the most repressed aspects of psyche imprisoned beneath the residue of hundreds of years of scientism and moralism. James Hillman in particular has moved psychology towards the recognition of psyche within our mortality and to an understanding that embraces our pathologies as manifestations of soul:

> Psychic existence is without the natural perspective of flesh and blood, so that pathologizing by taking events to death takes them into their ultimate meaning for soul. One has one's death, each his own, alone, singular, toward which the soul leads each piece of life by pathologizing it. (Hillman, 1975 p. 110).

Many others following Hillman's lead, have explored some of the darkest and most feared pathologies in search of soul and the lost feminine. These explorations have ventured into the realms of homosexuality, trauma, depression, incest, sadism, masochism and suicide, to name a few. Yet, I question whether this way of approaching the soul has accomplished much in terms of true feminism, or actual soul-making. Thomas Moore, in his book on sadism states what I believe to be the credo of archetypal psychology: "Inspired by dark eros, the libertine effects and sustains the mortificatio, helping the life narrative and complaint to break down into deep soul fantasy" (Moore, 1990, p. 148). This is the fantasy of the libertine working to liberate the feminine soul from the literalness of the world. It is an example of the bias of the father relation towards phallic meaning, which is wholly psychological, imaginal, and metaphoric. This comes at the expense of the feminine soul that is inextricably bound to the life narrative, to flesh and blood, and which may not need to be broken down and liberated by fantasy, but rather, may need to be liberated from the fantasy of liberation.

It seems that even the darkest, most taboo subjects can be safely explored so long as the exploration remains psychological. Moore, using an allusion to sadism suggests that "the therapist has to do what Sade himself did—remain in the prison of fantasy, cut off from life, so that imagination can be released" (Moore, 1990, p. 147). Literalism has become the shadow of archetypal psychology that insists upon an epistemology exclusively of the imagination. "If the therapist takes sides against the libertine," states Moore," then the imagination of the problem breaks down, and the therapy is left only with literal mechanics that are acted out within the literalistic split" (1990, p. 147). I perceive archetypal psychology to be caught within a double standard, a narcissistic split. On the one hand we have honored the soul in its many manifest forms of pathology. But on the other hand, we look past the literalness of the pathology for meanings which are wholly psychological. The great taboo of psychology has become "acting out", and yet we recognize that in pathologizing this is precisely what the soul is doing.

Psychology has the strength and the courage to examine the darkest aspects of human behavior, offering insight and connection to these aspects of ourselves that we would rather disown. To this end we owe depth psychology a great debt, but we must not forget that the courage of psychology to look into the shadowy aspects of human nature is contingent upon keeping the problems psychological. This is true for depth psychology as well as for psychologies based upon the medical model. Regardless of whether meaning is found between neurotransmitters and chemical imbalances, early object relations, or mythologies and archetypes, all the different psychological theories are similar in that their perspective has been constructed within the imagination. The main difference between depth psychologists and the psychologists who work from a medical model is that depth psychologists are aware that their work is metaphorical, whereas most other psychologists are convinced that their model is not descriptive but actual. All psychology finds meaning in the insights and relationships made possible within the imagination, and it must not be forgotten that this perspective exists because of the inherent biological weakness of the father relation and the imaginal possibilities created by the hermetic separation from the literal world/body.

There is danger, however, when we forget the fundamental vulnerability underlying this perspective from which we derive our insights and understanding. We become deluded into believing that our masculine imagination is autonomous, having little or no connection with the lived world. As a consequence, women have been forced to carry the feminine, the body and our biology that have been ignored in favor of the insights and the intellectual meanings of our psychologies. The feminine has an inherent connection to the earth and to our bodies and carries the constant reminder of our biological roots. Robert Romanyshyn states that "sexuality is the most potent and insistent reminder that our bodies matter, that we are material beings with needs, desires, and hungers which return us, with our soaring ambitions and intellectual dreams, to the earth" (1989, p. 150). According to Romanyshyn, the witch, the hysteric and the anorexic are all negative images in our history of the denial of our attachment to the world/body. Romanyshyn writes about the witch as an image of the repressed feminine:

> In her vigorous and flagrant sexuality, a sexuality which is imagined in relation to the figure of the devil, the witch carries what we would deny and overcome in our flight from the body, and continues to remind us of this denial. Overloading the body of the witch with the weighty demands of the flesh, we would fix that pernicious body with its corrupt and stinking sexuality over there, and thus distance ourselves from it and be rid of it (1989, p. 150).

I believe that most forms of acting out have become the witches of today. We have been given the impression that it is somehow possible to live an entirely psychological life, and thus the move away from abstraction to manifest action is discouraged and even forbidden. Only when the foundations of our cultural edifice are threatened is acting out encouraged, insofar as the police or military action will displace the threat against our preference for a predominantly psychological existence.

In Apuleius' tale of Psyche, Eros has fallen in love with Psyche and comes to her each night under the veil of darkness and they make love. Is this not the ideal behind most analytical psychologies, to be embraced by the gods in the sanctity of our imaginations? But for Psyche this is not enough, she needs to know her lover and she acts out and lights a candle; and so begins her woeful journey towards a substantiated love in the world and, ultimately, with the gods.

It is not my aim to attack the validity of psychology. Rather, I am stressing the importance of recognizing and honoring the actual material that substantiates the images within the phallic imagination. Not to recognize the dependence of the imagination on the literal things of the world is irresponsible and a further repression of the feminine. Even those dark subjects that archetypal psychologists have dared to explore are only valid insofar as they are actual, literal and being acted out somewhere. Our psychologies would not exist without our pathologies. Our fascination with these dangerous aspects of human nature arises out of our own capacity to actualize them. In The Bacchae (Vellacott, 1954, p. 220), Dionysus asks

Pentheus if he would like to witness the Bacchanalia to which
he is morally and principally opposed:

> Pentheus: Why yes; for that, I'd give a weighty sum of gold.
> Dionysus: What made you fall into this great desire to see?
> Pentheus: It would cause me distress to see them drunk with
> wine.
> Dionysus: Yet you would gladly witness this distressing
> sight?
> Pentheus: Of course—if I could quietly sit under the pines.

That we are fascinated by the very aspects of ourselves to
which we are morally opposed, is distressing. But as with Pentheus, within the distress is the fascination that leads us to
examine the perversities out there, because we subconsciously
recognize them within ourselves. The distress is an intimation
of the vulnerability of our moral and psychological stance
from which we judge human nature. The distress that leads us
to examine the perversions and pathologies that define the
field of psychology may be the stirring of the soul longing to
be acted out of the oppression of a predominantly psychological existence. In this respect *The Bacchae* is a metaphor of our
cultural situation. It suggests that if psyche's longing for embodied experience is not allowed to be acted out, not allowed
feminine participation in the lived world, then we will be led
by our distress into situations where we will be acted upon
unwittingly.

Wolfgang Giegerich suggests that "there has only been one
mode in all of known history in which the soul has been truly
able to access, or better, generate actuality. This was the sacrifice" (1993). Within most forms of acting out is the need to
access actuality and the unconscious need for sacrifice. As we
sit Pentheus-like on the perch of ideation and understanding,
are we not subconsciously aware of the sacrifice to which we
have been led? Giegerich presents us with the possibility that
in the past the sacrificial act was the "pivot between the im-
mediate and the actual natural life of the living creature, and
the cultural existence of man which is posited, mediated from

the outset" (1993). Perhaps it is no coincidence that western culture became more predominantly patriarchal and psychological in relation to the degree that actual sacrifice became sublimated. Ultimately, however, we must be led by our distress to the realization that all of our epistemologies, political, religious, scientific and philosophical, are inextricably linked to the sacrifice within the experience of mortality:

> Soul and consciousness are not natural, they are contranatural. They owe their existence to a revolution, to the logical negation of life, to the intrusion of death violently disrupting the continuity and intactness of the sphere of biological life (Giegerich, 1993).

In most 'primitive' cultures—including the Greek culture to which our psychology is so indebted—ritual and sacrifice were a means of actualizing mythology and the gods. Sacrifice was a means of recreating the inherent bond between the actual and the imaginal by willing their separation, and in turn giving life to soul and soul to life:

> Formally, the sacrificial blow performed the miracle of actually driving non-existing logos or soul into carnate actuality and of thereby giving body to bodiless logos or soul, making them real. The outrageous sacrificial blow cutting into the intactness of the living animal or human married, indeed, welded logos or soul to reality. Thereby simultaneously deposing human existence from biology as its primary basis of life and instead installing it in mind or psyche (Giegerich, 1993).

Perhaps today the many forms of acting out are compensatory for our lack of access to carnate actuality, the feminine, and its fundamental substantiation of our conceptual understanding. In this respect the need to act out of the father relation is not so much the breaking down of the imagination as it is the need for the substantiation of the imagination.

Literalism and unreflective acting out is a significant problem within our world and I do not mean to justify or ignore the suffering and the atrocities actually taking place. On some level, however, this is more than a problem that needs to be reimagined or reconstructed. The intrigue with the many different possibilities of acting out is the material which dominates our newspapers, books and our television programs. Much of our fascination with acting out may arise precisely because our psychologies, our gods, and our rituals have become intolerably hollow due to their lack of "world relation":

> Psychology, in its innocence took only the one abstracted half of the archaic heritage into account, the meaning and the image aspect of the beautiful myths and symbols, and believed itself entitled to claim, for this mere half, the name of reality of the psyche. Archetypes, as archetypes in themselves and images in an imagistic understanding, just as the platonic forms, are removed from all historical deeds and from the logical, but real, action of the soul. They are completely cleansed of blood and all traces of a violent act. Psychology's gods are paper tigers. They are immunized from the actual world relation of an age and a culture (Giegerich, 1993).

I am not suggesting (nor is Giegerich) a return of ritualized sacrifice as a way of bringing soul back into the world and of revitalizing our psychology. I am suggesting, however, that our psychologies do need revitalizing, and we must begin by perceiving the vulnerability of our cultural edifice and the father relation upon which it is built. This in turn leads us to the acceptance that a fundamental feminine link to reality is missing. Without this connection we must be "willing to uncompromisingly suffer the emptiness, meaninglessness, and unrealness that its missing entails" (Giegerich, 1993). It is important that we rediscover ways of acting out our psychologies, just as it has been so important to psychologize our many forms of acting out.

References

Euripides. *The Bacchae and Other Plays.* Trans. P. Vellacott. New York: Penguin, 1954.

Giegerich, W. "Killings: Psychology's Platonism and the Missing Link to Reality." *Spring 54*, 1993, pp. 5-18.

Hillman, J. *Revisioning Psychology.* New York: Harper and Row, 1975.

Moore, T. *Dark Eros: the Imagination of Sadism.* Dallas: Spring, 1990.

Pedraza, R. L. *Hermes and his Children.* Einsiedeln: Daimon Verlag, 1989.

Romanyshyn, R. *Technology as Symptom and Dream.* New York: Routledge, 1989.

Samuels, A. *The Plural Psyche: Personality, Morality and the Father.* New York: Routledge, 1989.

MEMORIES, DREAMS, OMISSIONS[1]

SONU SHAMDASANI

"This is such an important and intensely original book—I think it will have an enormous success and become a classic!"
—Richard Hull, 1960.[2]

*M*emories, Dreams, Reflections is commonly regarded as Jung's most important work, as well as being the most widely known and read. It has been taken as his final testament, for, as Gerhard Adler notes, "Nowhere else has the man Jung revealed himself so openly or testified to his crises of decision and the existence of his inner law."[3] Since Jung's death, it has been the preeminent source on his life and has spawned a plethora of secondary literature. In this study, my first omission will be the vast majority of this secondary literature, for reasons that will become clear. I hope to show that through a process that has had disturbing implications for the understanding of Jung, and his rightful location in twentieth century intellectual history, *Memories, Dreams, Reflections* is by no means Jung's autobiography.

Sonu Shamdasani lives in London and is the editor of Théodore Flournoy's *From India to the Planet Mars* (Princeton University Press, 1994) and co-editor of *Speculations after Freud: Psychoanalysis, Philosophy, Culture* (Routledge).

The existence of *Memories, Dreams, Reflections* has significantly delayed scholarly work on Jung. In her preface to her biographical memoir, which was one of the first to appear, Barbara Hannah writes that "...Jung's children were very much against anything biographical being written about their father, since they feel that all that is necessary has been said in his own *Memories, Dreams, Reflections*."[4] When Jung biographies came to be written, without exception they all relied heavily on the book, not only as a source of information, but also as the fundamental narrative structure of Jung's life. Thus Hannah writes of *Memories* that it "...will always remain the deepest and most authentic source concerning Jung."[5] So much has the prevalent understanding of Jung relied on this text that it is unlikely such understanding could change without a radical rereading of it.

From the outset, the significance of an autobiography by Jung was entailed by his own understanding of the nature of the psychological enterprise. Jung claimed as one of his central insights the notion of the "personal equation." He writes: "...philosophical criticism has helped me to see that every psychology—my own included—has the character of a subjective confession."[6] Regardless of whether one agrees with this notion, it is crucial in understanding Jung's psychology, for it clearly indicates how Jung understood his own psychology—and meant it to be understood.

Aside from a tantalising glimpse in a private seminar in 1925,[7] however, Jung did not publicly present his life story. From his own understanding of the significance of the theorist's biography, this lacuna presented perhaps the major impediment for an understanding of his work. In that same seminar, he candidly provides one rationale for this lacuna:

> All of this is the outside picture of the development of my book on the types. I could perfectly well say that this is the way the book came about and make an end of it there. But there is another side, a weaving about making mistakes, impure thinking, etc., etc., which is always very difficult for a man to make public. He likes to give you the finished

product of his directed thinking and have you understand that so it was born in his mind, free of weakness. A thinking man's attitude towards his intellectual life is quite comparable to that of woman toward her erotic life.

If I ask a woman about the man she has married, "How did this come about?" she will say, "I met him and loved him, and that is all." She will conceal most carefully all the little meannesses, and squinting situations that she may have been involved in, and she will present you with an unrivalled perfection of smoothness. Above all she will conceal the erotic mistakes she has made...

Just so with a man about his books. He does not want to tell of thesecret alliances, the *faux pas* of his mind. This it is that makes lies of most autobiographies. Just as sexuality is in women largely unconscious, so is this inferior side of his thinking largely unconscious in man. And just as a woman erects her stronghold of power in her sexuality, and will not give away any of the secrets of its weak side, so a man centers his power in his thinking and proposes to hold it as a solid front against the public, particulary against other men. He thinks if he tells the truth in this field it is equivalent to turning over the keys of his citadel to the enemy.[8]

In this remarkable statement, what Jung sees as the near impossibility of honesty, which "makes lies of most autobiographies," proves to be the major contraindication for entering upon such an endeavour. Clearly, Jung hadn't the slightest intention of 'turning over the keys of his citadel' to his enemies. In the years following this seminar, Jung consistently held to this position. In 1953, Henri Flournoy, the son of Jung's mentor, the Swiss psychologist, Théodore Flournoy, relayed to Jung the question of a Dr. Junod as to whether he had written an autobiography or intended to do one.[9] Jung replied:

I have always mistrusted an autobiography because one can never tell the truth. In so far as one is truthful, or believes one is truthful, it is an illusion, or of bad taste.[10]

When it came to *Memories*, had Jung latterly succumbed to an illusion, or to a severe lapse in taste? In a letter to his lifelong friend Gustave Steiner, Jung expressed his continued resistance to undertaking an autobiography, despite continued pressure:

> During the last years it has been suggested to me on several occasions to give something like an autobiography of myself. I have been unable to conceive of anything of the sort. I know too many autobiographies and their self-deceptions and expedient lies, and I know too much about the impossibility of self description, to give myself over to an attempt in this respect.[11]

Jung was no less sanguine concerning the possibility of a biography of his life. In reply to J. M. Thorburn, who had suggested that Jung should commission a biography of his life, Jung states:

> ...if I were you I shouldn't bother about my biography. I don't want to write one, because quite apart from the lack of motive I wouldn't know how to set about it. Much less can I see how anybody else could disentangle this monstrous Gordian knot of fatality, denseness, and aspirations and whatnot! Anybody who would try such an adventure ought to analyze me far beyond my own head if he wants to make a real job of it.[12]

How then did *Memories* come about? It initially arose out of the suggestion of a remarkable publisher, Kurt Wolff. At that time, Jung already had exclusive contracts with Routledge and Kegan Paul and the Bollingen Foundation. That another publisher managed to publish Jung's "autobiography" was quite a coup, though clearly one that Kurt Wolff was up to. In an article entitled "On luring away authors," Wolff writes:

> Every country in the world has strict laws about white-slave traffic. Authors, on the other hand, are an unprotected species and must look after themselves. They can

be bought and sold, like girls for the white-slave trade—
except that in the case of authors it is not illegal.[13]

To Richard Hull, Jung's translator, Kurt Wolff described
how:

> ...for several years he had tried to persuade Jung to write it
> [an autobiography], how Jung had always refused, and how
> finally he (Kurt) hit on the happy idea of an "Eckerfrau" to
> whom Jung could dictate at random, the Eckerfrau being
> Aniela Jaffé.[14]

In a letter to Herbert Read, Kurt Wolff wrote that in the last
analysis it was Aniela Jaffé who persuaded Jung to undertake
this task.[15] Due to the involvement of another publisher, the
book did not go down the same editorial channels as the rest
of Jung's work, which was to have significant consequences
for what ensued.

In her introduction to *Memories*, Aniela Jaffé writes:

> We began in the spring of 1957. It had been proposed
> that the book be written not as a "biography" but in the
> form of an "autobiography," with Jung himself as the narra-
> tor. This plan determined the form of the book, and my first
> task consisted solely in asking questions and noting down
> Jung's replies.[16]

When the book was published, its significance for the understanding of Jung was perceptively pointed out by Henri Ellenberger. He writes:

> Few personalities of the psychological and psychiatric
> world have been as badly understood as Carl Gustav Jung...
> It is precisely the interest of his *Autobiography* that it per-
> mits us to unify in a plausible fashion the disparate images
> which one made up till now of the life, personality and work
> of the founder of Analytical Psychology.[17]

However, as I shall argue, its very plausibility by no means diminished the misunderstandings surrounding the work of Jung, but escalated them to unforeseen proportions.

From the beginning, much was made of Jung's omissions. On the one hand, Jung was much criticised for the absence of any mention of his lifelong extramarital affair with Toni Wolff, of figures such as Eugen Bleuler and Pierre Janet, and the vexed issue of his alleged collaboration with the Nazis. It has been argued that Jung's omissions, for a psychologist who made the issue of subjective confession into the cornerstone of his psychology, were the mark of bad faith and intellectual dishonesty. Seriously, this charge continues to be used as an indictment of the Jungian movement.

On the other hand these self-same omissions have not only been defended but given a profound rationale. Aniela Jaffé writes:

> In Jung's memoirs the personalia are almost entirely lacking, to the disappointment of many readers... This criticism and the charge of Jung's "unrelatedness" were beside the point. His eye was always turned to the impersonal, the hidden archetypal; background which he was willing to reveal only so far as it concerned his own life.[18]

Some have argued that such omissions are justified because *Memories* inaugurated nothing less than a new chapter in the history of autobiography and of Western self-understanding—that of the new, 'inner' form of modern psychological autobiography, and that *Memories* is historically as significant as the *Confessions* of St. Augustine or of Rousseau.[19]

This reading, which can be conveniently called the canonization of Jung, is brought out by Kathleen Raine in her review, "A sent man," in which she simply states:

> Jung's life, even so fragmentarily revealed, invites comparison not with profane autobiography, but with the lives of Plotinus and Swedenborg, the lives of the saints and sages, interwoven with miracle.[20]

Raine was not the only one to make the comparison with the lives of saints. The same analogy was made by the psychologist Hans Eysenck, though with a characteristically different slant. In his review, he writes:

> Acolytes writing hagiographies are seldom fortunate enough to have the assistance of the saint himself in their endeavours; Aniela Jaffé had the benefit of extensive discussion with Jung... It may therefore be regarded as representing the kind of picture Jung wished to give of himself.[21]

In the prologue to *Memories*, Jung writes: "I have now undertaken...to tell my personal myth [den Mythus meines Lebens]." Thus the text itself was taken as a paradigmatic example of what such a myth might look like. In this way, it was not only taken as the definitive account of Jung's life, but also of the form that a psychologically individuated life should take. Edward Edinger comments:

> ...just as Jung's discovery of his own mythlessness paralleled the mythless condition of modern society, so Jung's discovery of his own individual myth will prove to be the first emergence of our new collective myth... Almost all the important episodes of Jung's life can be seen as paradigmatic of the new mode of being which is the consequence of living by a new myth.[22]

In her introduction to the book, Aniela Jaffé states that its genesis determined its eventual form. Hence a word or two is necessary concerning Aniela Jaffé and her relationship with Jung. Jaffé first encountered Jung in 1937 and subsequently went into analysis with him. Twenty years later, she became his secretary. It was a job she would be well suited to, as she had already worked as a freelance secretary for Professors Gideon and von Tsharner.[23] In 1947 she became Secretary of the Jung Institute in Zürich.

In an interview, she recalled that after his wife's death, Jung did not feel like answering his correspondence, and that she answered many letters in his name, reading him her replies, to which he at times made minor corrections.²⁴ This astonishing statement leaves unclear precisely how many of Jung's letters during this period were written in this fashion. Jung's late letters, which make up the bulk of the second volume of his selected letters, which Aniela Jaffé edited with Gerhard Adler, are commonly held to have his wisest and most humane statements. How many of these were actually the work of Aniela Jaffé?

This working arrangement shows the initial level of trust that Jung showed in Jaffé, allowing him to "write in his name." It further helps us understand how *Memories* was composed. At the outset, Jung trusted her ability to "assume his 'I,'" and to represent it to the outer world.

In her introduction to *Memories*, Aniela Jaffé states, "Jung read through the manuscript of this book and approved it."²⁵ Hence it has generally been taken that Jung was ultimately responsible for any omissions in the text. However, from the start, there were rumours of another order of omissions. This question was put to Jaffé in an interview with Suzanne Wagner which took place in 1977:

> Wagner: I heard that there were parts of his autobiography that were not allowed to be published—ideas about reincarnation for example.
> Jaffé: No, we published everything I thought could be published. What I cut were parts on the chapter he had written on Africa. It was simply too long. It would have taken the whole book. But I discussed it with him and he was very glad.²⁶

The only significant omission in the text would thus seem to be a booklength account of Jung's travels in Africa, which would be a lost continent of Jung's work, which has subsequently never surfaced. Be that as it may, what is crucial here is her statement that Jung approved of the changes that were made.

In a conversation in 1988 with Michael Fordham that was the instigation of my research, he spoke of his impressions of an early draft of *Memories* that he had read. He stated that the early chapters were greatly different and "far madder" than the published version. I subsequently located an editorial typescript at the Countway Library of Medicine at Harvard, and found not only whole chapters that were not published— such as an account of Jung's travels in London and Paris, and a chapter on William James—but also significant editing on almost every page.[27] I then contacted Aniela Jaffé concerning my research project. She informed me that not all of the material upon which the book was based went into the published text, and that she had planned to use some of the further material at a later date, but that permission was denied by the Jung heirs.[28] She informed me that the transcripts of the interviews were at the Library of Congress, which I subsequently consulted.[29]

I will first deal with some general features of the texts. While the Countway manuscript is recognizable as an extended version of the published text, the same is not true concerning the unpublished transcripts. Jaffé herself deals with the difference between the published texts and the actual interviews. Some had claimed that as she had been Jung's secretary, her task in compiling *Memories* had simply been to take down Jung's dictation. This claim incensed her, and led her to reveal the active role she had in fact had. In a letter, Jaffé noted that it was completely ridiculous to claim, as many did, that Jung had merely dictated to her. She noted that Jung spoke in something like a Freudian free association, and that his mode of speaking was not suitable for print. She noted that she had to do a great deal of work untangling these associations into a coherent narrative. Hence the view that the text was simply dictated represented a great compliment to her work.[30]

This statement reveals her active hand in the text, and suggests that the whole narrative structure of the book, which has been taken not only as the quintessence of Jung's life, but the exemplar of the new myth of individuation that the latter represented, was largely her construction. The typescripts themselves give a completely different impression. They usually begin with Jaffé posing specific questions and Jung associating freely in reply, following no chronological pattern. In a passage from the Countway typed manuscript that was omitted, Jung said that the frequent repetitions in the text were an aspect of his circular mode of thinking. He described his method as a new mode of peripetetics.[31] This suggests that in terms of narrative structure at least, something rather central to Jung's self-understanding landed up on the cutting floor.

In the published version, the paucity of any mention of figures in Jung's life is taken by some as the mark of his individuation or self-realization, and by others as a symptom of a quasi-autistic withdrawal from the world, or of an extreme degree of narcissism. However, in the typescripts of the interviews, there are many passages on figures as varied as Adolf Hitler, Billy Graham, Eugen Bleuler and Sabina Spielrein, not to mention a lengthy passage on the uncanny and suggestive resemblance between Jung's sister and Goethe's sister. I will first take up one such omission, as an example.

Many have waited with baited breath concerning Jung's lifelong extramarital affair with Toni Wolff; and yes, the transcripts do indeed contain material on this affair. Laurens van der Post justifies its omission as follows:

> She [Toni Wolff] is not mentioned in Jung's *Memories*, and one understands the omission in measure, because the book is a record only of quintessence. Jung's own personal relationships are deliberately not a part of it.[32]

Van der Post provides the following account of her role in his life:

> She was the only person capable of understanding, out of her own experience and transfiguration, what Jung was taking upon himself. This world of the unconscious which he was entering as a man, she had already endured as a woman. Thanks to Jung's guidance she had re-emerged, an enlarged and re-integrated personality.[33]

In this view, she plays the role of Beatrice in the Dantesque *Vita Nuova* that was Jung's myth. In the transcripts of Jaffé's interviews with Jung, he said that at the beginning of her analysis, Toni Wolff had incredible wild and cosmic fantasies, but because he was so preoccupied with his own, he was unable to deal with hers.

He said that he was faced with the problem of what to do with Toni Wolff after her analysis, which he ended, despite feeling involved with her. A year later, he dreamt that they were together in the Alps in a valley of rocks, and that he heard elves singing in a mountain into which she was disappearing, which he dreaded. After this, he contacted her again, as he knew that it was unavoidable, and because he felt in danger of his life. On a later occasion, while swimming, he found himself with a cramp, and vowed that if it receded, and he survived, he would give in to the relationship—which he then embarked upon. He said that he had infected her with his experience, which was awful and terrible, and that she got drawn into it and was equally helpless. He said that he became her centre, and through his insights, she found her centre. However, she needed him to play this role too much, which meant that he couldn't be himself, and she got lost. He felt as if he were being torn apart and often had to hold onto the table to keep together.

In this instance, one perhaps can understand the omission for reasons of propriety, but this is by no means so concerning the following omission. To contextualise it, I will address some critical differences between the published version and the Countway manuscript. In *Memories* the only section that is named after an individual is that on Freud, leaving the impression that the two most important figures in Jung's life were Freud and God, which has left commentators disputing which of these two came first. This impression is strengthened in the American and English editions, as the appendices on Théodore Flournoy and Heinrich Zimmer which are in the German edition are absent.[34] This strengthens the Freudocentric reading of Jung, which to date has been the prime manner that Jung and the development of Analytical Psychology have been understood.

The Countway manuscript presents a radically different organization. This version shows variant chapter arrangements that considerably alter the structure of the narrative. The section following the chapter on Freud is headed "Memories. Flournoy—James—Keyserling—Crichton   Miller—Zimmer." This heading is then crossed out by hand, and replaced by "Théodore Flournoy and William James."[35] These variations in arrangement alone show the contingency of the arrangement in *Memories*. Further, in this arrangement, the tributes to Flournoy and James directly follow the section on Freud.

In the chapter on Freud in *Memories*, Jung diagnoses Freud as suffering from a serious neurosis and claims that his followers have not grasped the significance of their founder's neurosis. For Jung, the universal claims made by Freud's psychology are invalid due to Freud's neurosis. The chapter that immediately follows portrays Jung's heroic "confrontation with the unconscious" and his discovery of archetypes, and through the discovery of his own myth, a means for "modern man to find his soul." *Memories* furthers the myth of Jung's heroic descent and self-generation, after he has freed himself from the shackles of Freudian psychology (founding a foundling psychology, without antecedents, with no prior model to follow, only counter exemplars).

The Countway typed manuscript presents a very different version. In the sections on Flournoy and James, which immediately follow the chapter on Freud, the problems as to how one could found a non-neurotic psychology, on which Jung claims Freud foundered, already appear to have been answered in the affirmative before Freud, by Flournoy and James. Further, Jung portrays the positivity of the mentoring relationship, through which no breaks were necessary. Jung credits their significance in helping him to formulate his criticisms of Freud and furnish the methodological presuppositions for his formulation of a post-Freudian psychology.[36]

In the chapter on James, Jung gives an account of their contact and attempts to spell out his intellectual debt to James. Jung recounts that he met James in 1909 and paid him a visit the following year. He said that James was one of the most outstanding persons that he ever met. He found him aristocratic, the image of a gentleman, yet free of airs and graces. He spoke to Jung without looking down on him; Jung felt that they had an excellent rapport. He felt that it was only with Flournoy and James that he could talk so easily, that he revered James' memory, and that he was a model. He found that both of them were receptive and of assistance with his doubts and difficulties, which he never found again. He esteemed James' openness and vision, which was particulary marked in his psychical research, which they discussed in detail, as well as his seances with the medium Mrs. Piper. He saw the far-reaching significance of psychical research as a means of access to the psychology of the unconscious. Jung said that he was also very influenced by James' work on the psychology of religion, which also became for him a model, in particular, by the way in which he managed to accept and let things stand, without forcing them into a theoretical bias.

These two omissions concern the large scale deletion of several critical figures in Jung's life. The third omission consists simply in a small detail, yet its implications for the understanding of the genesis of Jung's thought is perhaps no less significant. In a passage in *Memories* that has attracted much attention, Jung describes his experience of hearing the voice of a female patient speak within him, informing him that his activities were in fact art, and which he famously christened as the the voice of the anima. Subsequent to the publication of Aldo Carotenuto's *A Secret Symmetry*, it has generally been assumed that this patient was none other than Sabina Spielrein.

The most extended argument for this occurs in John Kerr's *A Most Dangerous Method*, where it forms a crucial part of a thesis that the most important intellectual and emotional influences on Jung were Freud and Spielrein. Kerr states: "The first mention of the 'anima' to occur in Jung's writings came in his 1920 tome *Psychological Types*."[37] (However, as noted long ago by the editors of the collected works, Jung had already treated of the anima in his 1916 "The structure of the

unconscious"[38] and *Psychological Types* was actually published
in 1921). Kerr claims that Jung "immortalised" Spielrein under the name of the anima, arguing that two clues Jung gave
as to the woman's identity—that he had been in correspondence with her, and that he broke with her in 1918-19,
point to Spielrein. However in the transcripts, where he actually speaks of Spielrein by name, Jung simply implies that he
lost touch with her when she went to Russia. Kerr claims
that: "Perhaps the biggest clue...is the debate on science ver-
sus art."[39] However, to make this last clue point to Spielrein,
Kerr claims, without any textual support, that the voice had
actually said, "It is not science. It is poetry."[40] Kerr's supposi-
tion that the voice was Spielrein leads him to "correct" the
historical record so that it supports his claim, forming a circular argument. Kerr also claims that Jung's stone carving at
Bollingen of a bear rolling a ball represents Spielrein, and
concludes that "Jung's 'anima,' the 'she who must be obeyed'
finished her career as a Freudian,"[41] thus substantiating his
Freudocentric reading of the genesis of Jung's psychology.
However, there are grounds for asserting that the stone carving does not represent Spielrein. Roger Payne notes that
"Franz [Jung] said that the often discussed bear which 'sets
the ball rolling' in his Bollingen carving was actually Emma
[Jung]."[42]

In the transcripts, Jung adds a small but telling detail—that
the woman in question was Dutch. The one Dutch woman in
Jung's circle at this time was Maria Moltzer.[43] The closeness of
her relationship to Jung is attested to by Freud. On December
23rd, 1912, in reply to Jung's letter of 18 December in which
Jung claimed that he had been analyzed, and hence was not
neurotic, unlike Freud who hadn't been,[44] Freud wrote to
Ferenczi: "The master who analyzed him could only have
been Fräulein Moltzer, and he is so foolish as to be proud of
this work of a woman with whom he is having an affair."[45]
Freud's claim is substantiated by Jolande Jacobi, who claimed
in an interview: "I heard from others, about the time before
he met Toni Wolff, that he had had a love affair there in the
Burgholzli with a girl—what was her name? Moltzer."[46] In an

unpublished letter of 1 August, 1918, Moltzer wrote to Fanny Bowditch Katz, who had been her patient,

> Yes, I resigned from the Club. I could not live any longer in that atmosphere. I am glad I did. I think, that in time, when the Club really shall become something, the Club shall be thankful I did. My resignation has its silent effects. Silent, for it seems that it belongs to my path, that I openly don't get the recognition or the appreciation for what I do for the development of the whole analytic movement. I always work in the dark and alone. This is my fate and must be expected.[47]

Jung subsequently made an acknowledgement to her, tucked away in a footnote in *Psychological Types*, where he states: "The credit for having discovered the existence of this type [the intuitive] belongs to Miss M. Moltzer."[48] Given that Jung regarded himself as of this type, this statement is telling. Taken together, I would claim that the case for the voice having been that of Moltzer is significantly stronger than for it having been Spielrein's.

At the current time, it is unclear who in a particular instance was responsible for a specific omission.[49] However, one might counter, that if Jung approved the changes, as Jaffé leads us to believe, these questions are not of great import. Crucial light on Jung's attitude to the text is shed by an unpublished memo written by Richard Hull, entitled, "A record of Events preceding Publication of Jung's Autobiography, as seen by R.F.C. Hull." Hull narrates that in February 1960, Jaffé informed him that Jung wanted to see him at the end of the month. Hull writes:

> The old man turned up...said he wanted to talk, and talked solidly for over an hour about the autobiography. I gathered that there was some controversy going on as to the "authentic" text. (At this time I had seen no text at all.) He impressed upon me, with the utmost emphasis, that he had said what he wanted to say in his own way—"a bit blunt and crude sometimes"—and that he did not want his work to be

tantifiziert ("auntified" or "oldmaidified," in Jack's felicitous phrase). "You will see what I mean when you get the text," he said. As he spoke at some length about the practice of "ghost-writing" by American publishers. I inferred that the "Tantifierung" would be done by Kurt. I thereupon asked Jung whether I would have the authority to "de-old maidify" the text supplied to me by Kurt. "In those cases," he said, "the big guns will go into action," pointing to himself. I found all this rather puzzling, because Kurt had said earlier that, especially in the first three chapters, the impact lay precisely in the highly personal tone and unorthodox outspokenness, which should at all costs be preserved.[50]

Hull then read the text and began revising the translation. He recounts:

It soon became apparent that the alterations were all of a kind which toned down and "old-maidified" Jung's original written text. As some of the deleted passages seemed to me extremely important for a proper understanding of the subsequent narrative, I restored them from Winston's version, together with a number of critical references to Jung's family, and some remarks which couldn't shock anyone, except the Swiss bourgeoisie, including a highly dramatic use of the word "shit." I suspected that the "auntie" was to be found not at the Hotel Esplanade in Locarno but nearer home in Kusnacht, and that it was Aniela Jaffé'.[51]

It seems that before Jung, the "big gun," could go into action, he died. After his death, Hull took up this issue directly with Jaffé. In reference to a proposed excision, he writes:

I would call the excision—and I choose my word very carefully—censorship, a thing that Jung would have despised and detested... Four times you have said that you are no longer capable of being objective. In a matter of such vital importance, dear Mrs. Jaffé, it is your duty to regain your objectivity: it was in your hands and no one else's, that Jung entrusted the responsibility for the final version of his life's testimony... Do you imagine that if Pantheon are compelled to bring out an expurgated edition, all this explosive evi-

dence is going to lie idle? ... All my arguments pale and di-
minish beside the one dominant thought: why did the old
man take the trouble to come to see me, and talk so ear-
nestly about the book, and why did he entrust it into your
hands? I must leave you to find the answer.[52]

However, Hull himself was reticent in how far he was willing
to go to "de-auntify" the text. In one section, Jung diagnosed
his mother as hysterical. This was omitted. In a letter to Gerald Gross, Hull writes:

> Aniela wrote that Mrs. Niehus would insist on its removal,
> and that this was Mrs. N.'s condition for Aniela's final
> placet... felt that it would be a blunder to antagonize her by
> fighting for the word "hysterical." To be frank, I am not
> willing to jeopardize my relations with her, as regard future
> work, for its sake. I therefore suggested "nervous" by way of
> a compromise, and Aniela gladly accepted this. At the same
> time, I have pointed out yet again that this little piece of
> family censorship will in all probability come to light in the
> end...[53]

The significance of these changes is that they concern the
manuscripts of the sections of *Memories* that Jung actually
wrote —and which have been the basis of an endless stream of
psychobiographies.

The final issue is that of the book's billing as Jung's autobiography. Hull highlighted the significance of this issue:

> ...there is all the difference in the world between a book ad-
> vertised as "The Autobiography of C. G. Jung" and a book
> of Jung's memoirs edited by Aniela Jaffé (of whom few have
> heard). One is an automatic bestseller, the other is not.[54]

As one would expect, Jung's English publisher, Routledge,
clearly wanted to publish the book. In a letter of 18 December
1959, Cecil Franklin wrote to Jung:

> I believe that the history of this book is that it started as a
> work by Aniela Jaffé which she would have written with

your close help; but that it grew out of that and far beyond it until it became in fact your autobiography... We have looked into our agreement for 1947 and find that if this is indeed your autobiography...publishing rights would be with us... We have looked forward to the time when we might publish your autobiography... It would worry us very much and might harm our reputation over here to be considered the publishers only of your more strictly technical books...[55]

However, Jung never regarded the book as his autobiography. On the 5th of April 1960, Jung wrote to Walter Niehus-Jung, his son-in-law and literary executor:

I want to thank you for your efforts on behalf of my so-called "Autobiography" and to confirm once more that I do not regard this book as my undertaking but expressly as a book which Frau A. Jaffé has written... The book should be published under her name and not under mine, since it does not represent an autobiography composed by myself.[56]

On the 25th of May, 1960, Herbert Read wrote to John Barrett concerning the book:

It now appears it will have some such title as :

Aniela Jaffé

"Reminiscences, Dreams, Thoughts"

with contributions from C.G. Jung.[57]

Following these negotiations, a resolution of the Editorial Committee of the Collected Works of Jung was drawn up, allowing the book to be published outside of the exclusive contracts with the Bollingen Foundation and Routledge and Kegan Paul. It contains the following statement:

C. G. Jung has always maintained that he did not consider this book as his own enterprise but expressly as a book written by Mrs. Jaffé. The chapters written by C. G. Jung were to be considered as his contributions to the work of Mrs. Jaffé. The book was to be published in the name of Mrs. Jaffé and not in the name of C. G. Jung, because it did not represent an autobiography composed by C. G. Jung (letter of C. G. Jung to Walter Niehus dated 5th April 1960).

On a conference held on the 26th August between Prof. C. G. Jung, Mr. John Barrett, Miss Vaun Gillmor, Sir Herbert Read, Mr. and Mrs. W. Niehus-Jung and Mrs. Aniela Jaffé, C. G. Jung confirmed again that he did strictly consider this book as an undertaking of Mrs. A. Jaffé to which he had only given his contributions... The Editorial Committee decides hereby formally that it will not approve any decision of the Executive Subcommittee which would add the book of Mrs. A. Jaffé to the Collected Works.[58]

From this, it appears that it was a precondition for the contractual release of the book that it appeared as Aniela Jaffé's biography of Jung, rather than as Jung's autobiography. In July, 1960, Kurt Wolff resigned from Pantheon, which was subsequently bought by Random House. On June 6th, 1961, Jung died. The following year, extracts from *Memories* appeared in *Die Weltwoche* and the *Atlantic Monthly*. The first extract in *Die Weltwoche* was simply titled, "The Autobiography of C.G. Jung." The book itself appeared in 1962 in English and German. In October of that year, Kurt Wolff died in a car crash. A French edition appeared in 1966, entitled, *My Life: Memories, dreams and thoughts*.[59]

What was indeed a remarkable biography has been mistakenly read as an autobiography. Unfortunately, it seems that when some grasped the significance of the confession of Jung's "personal equation," their efforts were in part directed towards determining the form it should take, and which of his memories and dreams to omit—fashioning Jung in their own likeness, making him the bearer of their "personal myths." Might it now be time for a de-auntification?

Notes

1. I am grateful to Michael Whan for this title.

2. Richard Hull to John Barrett, 4th May, 1960, Bollingen Archive, Library of Congress. Hull's letters have been cited with the permission of Mrs. Birte-Lena Hull.

3. Gerhard Adler, "The Memoirs of C. G. Jung," *The Listener*, July 18th, 1963, p. 85.

4. Barbara Hannah, *Jung: His Life and Work, A Biographical Memoir*, (London: Michael Joseph, 1976) p. 7.

5. *Ibid.*, p. 8.

6. Jung, "Freud and Jung: Contrasts," *CW* 4, p. 336.

7. Jung, *Analytical Psychology: Notes of the Seminar given in 1925*, *CW* Supplementary Volume.

8. *Ibid.*, pp. 32-3.

9. Henri Flournoy to Jung, 8th February, 1953, Jung archives, E. T. H., Zürich.

10. Jung to Henri Flournoy, *C. G. Jung Letters* vol 2: 1951-1961, ed., Gerhard Adler and Aniela Jaffé, (London: Routledge and Kegan Paul, 1976), p. 106, translation modified. In a dedicatory note to a collection of his offprints for Jürg Fierz, Jung simply wrote: "I myself have a distaste for autobiog-raphy." 21st December, 1945, *C. G. Jung Letters*, vol. 1: 1906-1950, (London: Routledge and Kegan Paul, 1973), p. 404.

11. Jung to Gustave Steiner, 30th December, 1957, *C. G. Letters* Vol. 2., p. 406, trans. modified.

12. Jung to J. M. Thorburn, 6th February, 1952, *C. G. Jung Letters 2: 1951-1961*, pp. 38-39.

13. Kurt Wolff, "On Luring Away Authors, or How Authors and Publishers Part Company," *Kurt Wolff: A Portrait in Essays and Letters*, ed. M. Ermarth, (Chicago, University of Chicago Press, 1991), p. 21.

14. Richard Hull, "A record of events preceding the publication of Jung's autobiography, as seen by R. F. C. Hull," July 27th, 1960, Bollingen archive, Library of Congress. Cited with permission, Mrs. Birte-Lena Hull. In her introduction to *Memories*, Aniela Jaffé states that it was Jolande Jacobi who suggested her for this role. The Eckermann-Goethe analogy was not lost on Jung; in a letter to Kurt Wolff, he wrote, "God help me, when I read Eckermann's *Conversations* even Goethe seemed to me like a strutting turkey-cock." Jung to Kurt Wolff, 1st February, 1958, *C. G. Jung Letters*, Vol 2., p. 453.

15. Kurt Wolff to Herbert Read, October 27th, 1959, Bollingen archive, Library of Congress.

16. Jung, *Memories, Dreams, Reflections*, (London: Flamingo, 1983), p. 7.

17. Henri Ellenberger, "La Psychologie de Carl Gustav Jung: à Propos de son Autobiographie," *L'Union Médicale du Canada*, vol. 93, August 1964, p. 993, trans. mine.

18. Aniela Jaffé, *From the Life and Work of C. G. Jung*, (Einsielden: Daimon, 1989), p. 133.

19. One of the first to make these analogies was Arthur Calder-Marshall, in his review, "Jung: the Saint of Psychology," *Time and Tide*, 11th-17th July, 1963, in which he stated: "This volume...is destined to be as much a classic as Rousseau's *Confessions*." p. 24.

20. Kathleen Raine, "A Sent Man," *The Listener*, 22nd August, 1963, p. 284.

21. Hans Eysenck, "Patriarch of the Psyche," *The Spectator*, July 19th, 1963, p. 86.

22. E. Edinger, *The Creation of Consciousness: Jung's Myth for Modern Man*, (Toronto: Inner City Books, 1984), pp. 12-13.

23. Aniela Jaffé, interview with Gene Nameche, Jung oral history archive, Countway Library of Medicine, Harvard Medical Library, Boston, p. 11.

24. *Ibid.*

25. Jung, *Memories, Dreams, Reflections*, p. 9.

26. Suzanne Wagner, "Remembering Jung: through the eyes of Aniela Jaffé," *Psychological Perspectives*, vol. 26, 1992, p. 109.

27. Dr. Richard Wolff, whom I would like to thank for facilitating my researh, informed me that one of the editors involved in the publication sold it to a bookseller. It was then purchased by Dr. James Cheatham and donated to the Harvard Medical Library in May 1979. It bears corrections by several hands, some of which were identified by Alan Elms: Gerald Gross, Aniela Jaffé (through Richard Winston), Richard Hull, Wolfgang Sauerlander, Richard Winston, together with notes labelled 'CGJ,' though not in Jung's hand.

28. Aniela Jaffé to the author, letter dated January 1991. All statements from her letters and from the manuscripts, drafts and transcripts are given in paraphrase, as permission to quote has not been granted by the executor of the Jaffé estate.

29. The transcripts, together with some correspondence concerning their fate, were officially restricted until 1993; I thank William McGuire and Princeton University Press for allowing me to consult them in the Easter of 1991.

30. Aniela Jaffé to William McGuire, 1981, Bollingen archive, Library of Congress.

31. Countway ms., p. 1.

32. Laurens van der Post, *Jung and the Story of our Time* (London: Penguin, 1976), p. 172.

33. *Ibid.*, p. 176.

34. Jung's tribute to Flournoy is published in English in Théodore Flournoy, *From India to the Planet Mars: A Case of Multiple Personality with Imaginary Languages*, ed. Sonu Shamdasani, (Princeton: Princeton University Press, forthcoming 1994). Jung's tributes to Flournoy and Zimmer were also published in the French edition of *Memories*.

35. Countway ms., p. 197.

36. For Jung's relation to James, see Eugene Taylor, "William James and C. G. Jung," *Spring* 1980; For a complementary critique of the Freudocentric

reading of Jung, see his "Jung in His Intellectual Setting: The Sweden-borgian Connection," *Studia Swedenborgiana*, Vol 7, 1991.

37. John Kerr, *A Most Dangerous Method: The Story of Jung, Freud and Sabina Spielrein*, (New York: Knopf, 1993), p. 503. It is curious that Kerr did not draw upon Spielrein's case history, despite the fact that it has been in the public domain since 1992 in Bernard Minder's "Sabina Spielrein: Jungs Patientin am Burghoelzli," (Ph.D, University of Bern, 1992). (I thank Han Israëls for alerting me to this, and suppling a copy.) Need less to say, this material, together with the letters between Bleuler, Jung and Spielrein's family that Minder has retrieved, occasions a complete re-evaluation of the Jung-Spielrein relationship. The draft letter of referral from Jung to Freud concerning Spielrein in 1905 that Minder has retrieved ("Jung an Freud 1905: Ein bericht über Sabina Spielrein," *Gesnarus* vol. 50, 1993), brilliantly confirms Peter Swales's reconstruction in "What Jung *Didn't* Say," *Harvest: Journal for Jungian Studies*, Vol. 38, 1992. For further new material on Spielrein, see my "Spielrein's Associations: A Newly Identified Word Asso-ciation Protocol," *Harvest: Journal for Jungian Studies*, Vol. 39, 1993.

38. *CW* 7, p. 295, n. 21.

39. *Op. cit.*, p. 506.

40. *Op. cit.*, p. 507.

41. *Ibid.*

42. Roger Payne, "A visit to 228 Seestrasse," *Harvest: Journal for Jungian Studies*, Vol. 39, 1993, p. 137.

43. William McGuire provides the following biographical information on Moltzer: "Mary or Maria Moltzer (1874-1944), daughter of a Netherlands distiller, became a nurse as a protest against alcoholic abuse. Had Psycho-analytic training with Jung and after 1913 continued as an analytical psy-chologist." Ed. William McGuire, *The Freud/Jung Letters* (London: Hogarth/Routledge, 1974), pp. 351-2. For Moltzer's role as Jung's assistant, see Eugene Taylor, "C. G. Jung and the Boston Psychopathologists, 1902-1912," *Voices*, Vol. 21, 1985.

44. *Ibid.*, p. 535.

45. Ed. E. Brabant, E. Falzeder & P. Giampieri-Deutsch, *The Correspon-dence of Sigmund Freud and Sándor Ferenczi*, vol 1., 1908-1914, (Cambridge: Harvard University Press, 1993), p. 446.

46. Jolande Jacobi, interview with Gene Nameche, Jung oral history ar-chive, Box 3, p. 110, Countway Library of Medicine, Harvard Medical Li-brary, Boston.

47. Maria Moltzer to Fanny Bowditch Katz, 1st August, 1918, Countway Library of Medicine, Harvard Medical Library, Boston, cited with permis-sion.

48. *CW* 6, p. 454.

49. This issue has been explored in an excellent piece by Alan Elms, "The Auntification of Jung" in *One Life at a Time: Explorations in Psychobiog-*

raphy (forthcoming, Oxford University Press), which complements the discussion here.

50. Hull, "A record of events," pp. 1-2.

51. *Ibid.*, p. 2.

52. Richard Hull to Aniela Jaffé, Sept. 9, 1961, Bollingen archive, Library of Congress.

53. Richard Hull to Gerald Gross, Bollingen Archive, Library of Congress.

54. Hull, "A record of events," p. 4.

55. Cecil Franklin to C. G. Jung, 19th December, 1959, Bollingen archive, Library of Congress.

56. Jung to Walther-Niehus Jung, 5th April, 1960, *C. G. Jung: Letters*, vol. 2., p. 550, trans. modified.

57. Herbert Read to John Barrett, 25th May, 1960, Bollingen archive, Library of Congress.

58. "Resolution of the Editorial Committee for 'The Collected Works' of Prof. C. G. Jung," Bollingen archive, Library of Congress, signed by Jung on 29th November, 1960, and by John Barrett on 13th December, 1960.

59. "Die Autobiographie von C. G. Jung," *Die Weltwoche*, 31st August, 1962. The German title differs from the English: *Erinnerungen, Träume, Gedanken von C. G. Jung*, aufgezeichnet und herausgegeben von [recorded and edited by] Aniela Jaffé, (Olten: Walter Verlag, 1988). Other items in the German edition that were missing in the English editions were a letter by Jung to a 'young student,' Jung's postscript to his *Red Book* and "Details about C. G. Jung's family" by Aniela Jaffé. The latter item was published in English in *Spring*, 1984. There are many discrepancies between the German and English editions, notably numerous passages in the former that are missing from the latter. Some, but by no means all, were published in English by Shoji Muramoto, "Completing the Memoirs: The Passages Omitted or Transposed in the English and Japanese Versions of Jung's Autobiography," *Spring*, 1987. However, given that the text was being translated into English as it was being compiled, it is not possible to consider one or the other as the original version. The French edition was *Ma vie. Souvenirs, rêves et pensées*, recueillis et publiés par Aniela Jaffé, (Paris: Gallimard, 1966), trans. Roland Cahen and Yves Le Lay. Details concerning Kurt Wolff are from William McGuire, *Bollingen: An Adventure in Collecting the Past*, (Princeton: Princeton University Press, 1982), pp. 273-4 (I thank Charles Boer for recalling this to my attention).

LETTERS TO THE EDITOR

To the Editor:

Hillman's response in *Spring 56* to my article on "Killings" in *Spring 54* is an odd piece. In his introduction he calls my thought "so thoroughly radical..." and "the most imprtant Jungian thought now going on.," but then, in the body of his article, he accuses me of such basic fallacies that I look rather stupid. Either I am a radical thinker, and cannot be guilty of these fallacies, which for anyone in archetypal psychology are "elementary, dear Watson," because they have been discussed over and over again during the last twenty years. Or I am guilty of these fallacies, in which case why "urge each reader of what follows to read and take fully to heart Giegerich's remarkable pages in *Spring 54*"? Those pages just wouldn't be worth such attention, because Hillman's diagnosis, if correct, would simply be devastating for my entire piece.

Of course, Hillman was right in urging the reader to go back to my article and take it to heart. It is truly radical in that it questions some of the premises on which archetypal psychology rested (and with which it rested content) and in trying to push this psychology's frontier a bit forward. What is wrong is his diagnosis. Indeed, it can easily be shown that Hillman's charges are untenable. In part they attack an opponent that is not I, but an imaginary figure resulting from a prior misconstruction and misrepresentation of my arguments (e.g., when he claims that I use the past as a model for the present and "call for something concrete, like killing of animals"—a preposterous charge). In part Hillman is himself guilty of those fallacies that he believes he finds in my paper. Small example: When from the statement that the Gods are immortal (which I accept as correct) he concludes that the Greek Gods cannot be obsolete, he takes "immortal" as a literal fact rather than an imaginal attribute and is thus guilty of a "misplaced concretism." In part he is inconsistent, because he does not follow through with his own approach and eat his own medicine. Thus he wantsto base his psychology on Jung's idea that the psyche creates reality every day and on Hölderlin's idea that "Poetically man lives upon the earth," but when it comes to the topic of sacrifices, he deprives them of their poetic nature and their origin from the soul, refusing to see that the act of sacrifice, *as* literal act, contained within itself a wealth of imaginal or logical life of the soul, and was in itself an act of the soul's *poiesis*, one of the main ways in which fantasy originally created reality.

This was what I had tried to show; I had tried to uncover the "poem" or myth hidden in the act of sacrifice, thereby attempting to end the untenable, but still operative split between the literal and the imaginal. Hillman *malgré lui* insists on a non-poetic, positivistic understanding of rituals as *merely* literal fact requiring an *additional* act of imagination to become psychologically significant...

Here I regret that the editors of *Spring* did not want to print my ten-page response to Hillman's charges, on the grounds that they "decided not to continue the dialogue" because they "prefer new and separate articles over long-standing dialogues." I certainly appreciate their dilemma arising from being overwhelmed with manuscripts to be considered for publication. Nevertheless, it would have been better not to limit me to a short Letter to the Editor comment, for three reasons. First, what Hillman writes, as the Senior Editor of this journal, as the founding father of archetypal psychology, as the persuasive, eloquent stylist that he is, and as a kind of mythical figure already during his lifetime, has so much weight that it deserves closer scrutiny and a thorough demonstration that his accusations are untenable (rather than my mere lump-sum *assertion* above). Secondly, in his piece Hillman said that the contest was necessary. It would have made for a better contest, or it would have begun to *be* a real contest, if I as the other combatant would have been allowed into the ring too, rather than being constrained to do a little heckling from among the ranks of the audience in the way of a Letter to the Editor. Thirdly, if it's a question of new articles it could be worthwhile to make a distinction between "newness" in the sense of news items and "newness" in the sense of a new level of reflection. Then my response, even though it covers the same ground once more, could qualify as a new article, new at least for a consciousness for which Hillman's argumentation in his critique of my article on "Killings" represents the state of the art. Because my response carefully spells out the pitfalls in his argumentation and shows that his critique, rather than meeting the challenge of my article, tries to hold its theses down to the conventional thought patterns of archetypal psychology as we have known it all along.

Wolfgang Giegerich,
Stuttgart, Germany

[Editor's Note: The decision not to continue the dialogue between Giegerich and Hillman was made by the Editor, Charles Boer, not the Senior Editor. We consider Dr. Wolfgang Giegerich one of our eminent

contributors, and always look forward to publishing more of his work. But The Spring Journal now receives over a thousand manuscripts a year for consideration, and almost all of them are interesting theses, offering different levels of reflection. We feel that to be responsible to archetypal psychology on all its levels, we have to forego long-standing dialogues that can be accomodated in other ways.]

To the Editor:

Thank you for the review of my book [The Soul of the Law], in Spring 56. I was especially taken with the quote you chose ["Law firms are told they must get 'lean' by getting rid of the 'fat.' It's as if there is no room for voluptuousness, sensuality, comfort, warmth in the economic work place."] There is a story to go with it.

The quote uses the word "voluptuousness" with regard to an imagined work environment. The quote itself is part of a larger piece on workaholism that was excerpted in the American Bar Association Journal. However, the editors refused to print the word "volutpuousness" in the ABA Journal! They said it was too sexual (I swear I'm not making this up) and insisted that I change the word, suggesting that I use "generosity" instead. What a hoot. I agreed because (1) I needed the money, and (2) I find it very funny that they imagine voluptuosness" and "generosity" as synonyms. I figured what the hell, I'd get to use the right word in the book, and now look here—that word finds a way to get another caress by people who appreciate it.

Benjamin Sells,
Chicago, Illinois

To the Editor:

In his reply to Richard Noll in *Spring 56*, Greg Mogenson states that Noll inflates the significance of the fact, first noted by Henri Ellenberger, that the field of 19th century scholarship was a budding grove of solar phalli

> ...by quoting his colleague Sonu Shamdasani's view that this patient 'carries on his shoulders the weight and burden of proof of the Collective Unconscious' (p. 53). While this patient's back may be broken by the cumulative weight of Noll's and Shamdasani's findings, Jung did have other evidence of a collective unconscious. (p. 152)

However, the passage in question, from my "A Woman Called Frank" in *Spring 50*, actually stated:

> The Solar Phallus Man, *together with other figures*, carried on his shoulders the weight of the burden of proof of the Collective Unconscious. In this exemplum, by ruling out the role of cryptomnesia, Jung argued that the mythic hints, echoes, allusions, and textures that weave through our lives were traces or citations that did not stem from any putative origin within the shawl of one's lifetime. (italics added, p. 40)

Is Mogenson's comment a case of cymptomnesia, miscitation, recitation of a miscitation, or an undecidable combination of the three? Needless to say, citation should not be taken as a sign of understanding, nor for that matter, of collegiality.

"A Woman Called Frank" (which was taken up with the violence of framing and reframing) attempted to refashion the figural basis of Jung's psychology, and to shift the debate from the sterile alternation of debunking and defending, by reconceiving what formed the intimate support and conditions of possibility of Jung's reading yet at the same time remained occluded by it, and allowing it another hearing.

Sonu Shamdasani,
London, England

I WANT MY MONEY BACK

SHEILA GRIMALDI-CRAIG

Richard Noll, *The Jung Cult*. Princeton: Princeton UP, 1994. Pp. 387. $24.95, cloth.

This book has two axes to grind: one that Jung was a charismatic Nietzschean, immersed in occultism, who succeeded in creating a neo-pagan cult with himself as the high priest and god, and two, that he perpetrated this irrational cult as if it were a scientific psychology, which the cult members continue to this day because a) they are still naively dominated by his charismatic personality, and b) they are greedy for all the money that can be made by constantly expanding the cult. The book is written, from beginning to end, as an *exposé* of the Jung cult, though it bears three blurbs on the back cover from professors at Yale, Cornell, and Tufts, all trying to sell it as "the historical Jung," and claiming that the book "marks the entry of serious scholarly interest in the meaning of Jung's cultural constructions."

Academic stuff and nonsense, I say. *Whose* historical Jung? The professors *really* like this book because it tries to demolish everything that Jung contributed to psychology and to

Sheila Grimaldi-Craig taught for many years in the Connecticut Public Schools. She is now a regular reviewer for this journal.

culture. Well, they will read what they want, as always, and declare it to be history, especially since there are 77 pages of footnotes with plenty of Germanic references ("exceptionally, almost universally, well-read in the field of post-Enlightenment German-language culture and thought," one of the blurbs adds). Jungians will probably not read the book because, like professors, they, too, only tend to read what they like to hear, and Jungians are not going to like what they hear here. The irony is that the book is designed more to goad Jungians than to please anti-Jungians. It will do both.

Noll pretends he does not understand why there are so many more Jungians out there than Freudians. "Freud may be the genius of choice for the learned elite of the late twentieth century," he writes, "but it is clear that, in sheer numbers alone, it is Jung who has won the cultural war and whose works are more widely read and discussed in the popular culture of our age." While Freudianism "has enjoyed an exalted place in the pantheon of medicine," he adds, "Jung and his theories have remained well outside the established institutional worlds of science and medicine, as they have been regarded, with justification, as inconsistent with the greater scientific paradigms of the twentieth century." This leads to the question on which the whole book then sets out to give an answer: "Something else must account for the widespread popularity of Jung, but what?"

Noll knows damn well what: people—dupes, in his eyes—like me. "While its practitioners and theoreticians," he writes scornfully, "cite its legitimacy as a fruitful psychological theory and a profession of psychotherapy, the far greater number of participants in the movement who are not professionals are attracted by its 'spirituality.'"

I am neither a practitioner nor a theoretician, neither an analyst nor a therapist. (I hope nobody thinks my book reviews constitute Jungian theory—I only write them out of pique and amusement.) The analysts and therapists and practitioners should write their own replies to this book—and I hope they do, instead of just complaining or taking the usual superior position that the author has a problem.

So, yes, I am one of the vast majority attracted by Jungian "spirituality." (Noll makes it sound like a bad word.) I taught high school science (biology) for too many years to too many American kids, but I am the first to admit that there has to be more to life than the matter-of-fact, here-today, gone-tomorrow, "We-all-live-in-a-material-world-and-I'm-a-material-girl" sort of mentality. I am one of the vast majority who think Jung's "occultism" was in fact his best stuff. (I like Nietzsche, too, but Jung feels more contemporary.) From the Eleusinian mysteries of the Greeks to the Mithras cult rituals of Jung himself, I enjoy this kind of imaginative psychological play. I like to read about it anyway. I like to think that such fantasy has helped keep me sane (if this is what sane is). I did not, and do not, want a religion. I was raised a Roman Catholic, which is maybe why I like myths and rituals so much, but I couldn't abide the right-wing patriarchalist ideology that you had to accept as well, and Catholicism was *so* hard on women!

I don't mind the word "occult," though I know it has bad connotations in the science community vocabulary book. It always has. When I talk about this stuff with my husband, Douglas, who is a civil engineer, I use the word "imaginative," and sometimes the word "poetic," instead of the word "occult" to describe my interest and what I'm doing.

And what am I doing? I am imagining myself as part of a world which is still spiritually alive to the goddesses and gods of old, a world where I can hear nature itself breathing and speaking and crying out over oilspills and deforestations, a world of rapes and ruthlessness, crimes and passions that make sense only against a mythical reading of pathology, but a world that is marvelous and singing still with no less of the mystery of life (and some of the misery, too) than Greeks and Hebrews, Celts and Polynesians, Romans and Mayans imagined they heard here once upon a time. I have not been able to find that kind of vision in Freud or philosophy departments, and least of all in the spiritual dullness of "psychological science" today. (I love reading Darwin, too, and E. O. Wilson's ants are such fantastic little creatures I almost want to keep them around the house as pets!) I have

only found it in Jung and the Jungians, though not in all of
them by any means and sometimes not even in them.

So Richard Noll really ticks me off when he puts it like this:

> One of the selling points in the marketing of Jungian analy-
> sis today was also one of its attractions to the spiritual elit-
> ism of Jung's early contemporaries: the idea of analysis as
> initiation into mysteries...A descent into the depths is still
> today a favorite buzzword of Jungism...When Jung says
> that, "artificial aids have always been needed to bring the
> healing forces of the unconscious into play. It was chiefly
> the religions that performed this task," he is admitting the
> usurpation of the authority of the world's great religions to
> heal the spiritually bankrupt and, therefore, the legitimate
> dispensation of these sacraments by cults like his own.

Well speak for yourself, Richard Noll. Your previous book
was an enthusiastic study of vampires! The world's great religions know full well that they have lost the ball in the twentieth century, especially with people who can read. They have
become little more than battlegrounds in Northern Ireland,
in Israel, in the former Yugoslavia, in Islam everywhere, in
India and Sri Lanka. In the U.S. alone their exponents shoot
abortion doctors, imprison suicide doctors, beat up gays, censor books and mock women's rights. It is religion that is
spiritually bankrupt, even psychopathic, and the problem is
what do the rest of us do in the meantime, in the absence of
religion? Do we merely live out our lives in the smug, scien-
tistic, soulless corridors of academe?

Noll's point is that Jung tried to foist himself off as the new
god in the new religion and that his "followers" have simply
traded in "the world's great religions" for the not-so-great cult
of Jung. Suffering succotash, as Bugs Bunny used to say. Isn't
it time the academic critics retired these old canards? (E.
Glover was saying this in the 1940s in a book called *Freud or
Jung?*)

And get this:

Describing the contemporary Jungian movement as a form of personal religion implies that individual decision making plays a key role in determining how involved an individual may become with activities in groups that all have, almost without exclusion, spiritual or religious interests at heart. Although all are united by a common belief in individuation and a transcendent, transpersonal collective unconscious that is said to manifest itself through the individual psyche, the emphasis remains on the personal experience of the universal in the particular. This may be sought through contact with established Jungian social organizations or functionaries or through private visionary exercises, the reading of Jungian material, and self-reflection. The entire pantheon of all the world's mythologies, torn out of any semblance of its original cultural contexts, is utilized as an "objective" reference point for the interpretation of personal experience (a difficulty Lukács noted in all forms of Lebensphilosophie).

Do we all have to read mythology like Wendy Doniger, pretending that none of it relates to us and that it is only a culture-bound phenomenon that must never be taken out of context, especially as that context is defined for us by Professor So and So? Bullfeathers! Of course we tear mythology out of its original cultural context when we apply it to our own lives and personal experiences. What does Noll think the Romans did to the Greeks, the Hebrews to the Canaanites, the Greeks to the Egyptians? We live now, and these cultures are all part of *our* cultural context. We have every right in the world to read myths—or poems, fictions, and yes even history books—in whatever way they make sense to us. And please—please—no more Lukács quoting! Now that the Berlin Wall is down, and the Communists lost, can we please stop citing their favorite authoritarian ideologue professors as if they had some special purchase on truth.

Noll's problem is that he seems to have missed the revolution that came along even in academic thought a few years back, a revolution that tore to shreds the pretense that there is any objectivity when it comes to declaring truths in the humanities. It was called "Deconstruction" in one of its stages, the "New Historicism," in another, "Semiotics" in yet another. Whatever the approach, it was agreed that signs and symbols, words and ideas could be read in many ways, with no one claiming ultimate truth anymore or absolute objectivity or definitive statement.

That is what I find so quaint about the quest for "the historical Jung" that this book is supposed to be the harbinger of. Even the theologians began to give up on "the historical Jesus" around the 1960s, when they realized it was a losing proposition. Ditto "the historical Freud" that so many people thought they were establishing in the 1970s and 80s. Today Freud studies are more arrayed (and dismayed) than ever, and their hero interpreted, as he should be, in wildly varying ways.

Take, as an example, a subject I seem to have to defend in all my book reviews—because it is a subject dear to me—the role of women in the early Jungian movement and the continuing attractiveness for women of a Jungian point of view. Noll's twist on the phenomenon would have you believe that the original Jungians—Hinkle, Harding (Noll calls her, derogatively, "the *mater magna* of American Jungism"), Mann, Bertine, Wickes, Nordfeld, and Whitney—were a band of Dionysiac crazies. "Like the Dionysiac cults of antiquity," he writes, "the Jung cult seems to have started (and then prospered) as primarily a cult of women." Because "cult" is his hook, the lens through which he wants to read history and especially the history of the Jungian movement, there can be no other reason or explanation for these women's behavior than their cult madness. Even Mary Mellon, the benefactor of the Bollingen Foundation which published Jung's books, is part of the frenzied pack because she and her husband enabled the "sacred texts" to be produced.

These women (or *Those Women* as Nor Hall calls them in her much more sympathetic study of them) were not only the first Jungian analysts in the United States, several of them were also in the first generation of women medical doctors. They were intelligent and sensitive people, and for their own private emotional reasons—entirely understandable to me, I might add—wanted psychological help with their lives. They were drawn to Jung because his psychology did not demean or insult women the way Freud's did, and does. There were really no other choices at that time if you were a sophisticated and educated woman with an interest in medicine. Of course they were in awe of Jung. Of course he overpowered them with his theories and analysis. Of course they came away committed to his ideas for life. But they also became, as a result, terrifically forceful individuals—by every account I have ever read—who made valuable contributions to the psychological health of the city of New York (and elsewhere), establishing clinics and mental health centers at a time when Bellevue was the grim and only alternative. I am not going to go into their personal histories here—again—only to add that I really hate the kind of cheap slam these ladies always seem to get today from our new historians, who think that just because these ladies, many of whom were lesbians, could be bitchy and disagreeable sometimes, they can be lumped together indiscriminately as part of a band of hysterical old maids. If they were a Dionysiac cult, why not call them as well a "lesbian clique," or even early "femi-Nazis" (as Rush Limbaugh would encapsulate them if he were writing their "history")? The slant is everything.

Noll wants the Dionysiac cult metaphor because *his* Jung is Dionysus, or Mithras, and because Jungian analysis in his view can be rendered like this: "Starting in the late 1910s and throughout the 1920s, it was clear that to become a member of the secret church one must undergo a subterranean initiation in the mystery grotto of the collective unconscious in Switzerland—and for a fee."

Fees and money are a big part of Noll's attack on Jung and Jungians. At one point he calls it a "marketing pyramid" where you "buy a distributorship" with "individuation as the vague product sold" and with the psychoanalysts at the top collecting most of the fees, then therapists and others, down presumably to authors. He goes on and on with the money complaint, and in some ways it's at the heart of this book. As I don't get a nickel for writing this review, I'm certainly not going to defend such capitalist pigs, and I know you rich analysts out there who might be reading this will probably not defend yourselves either. (You're too busy with your broker.) But he's not just attacking high fees. He's saying that your psychology is nothing but a cult scam whereby the cult leaders make a lot of money off a foolish public.

> Charismatic exuberance becomes bureaucratized, and Dionysian spontaneity is replaced by Apollonian regimentation. The process of routinization reduces dependence on the direct authority of the charismatic leader. Although the seeds of this process are almost always present while the charismatic leader is at his strongest, usually the routinization is hastened by the incapacitation of the leader through sickness, age, or death. Association with a divinely inspired charismatic leader then becomes a major vehicle for material and economic gain when the leader's charisma is institutionally, rather than supernaturally, conferred on the elect.

Throughout the book, Jung is called "charismatic leader" so often that by the end you are convinced that this is the greatest cult manipulation of people in the 20th century. There is much talk, too, of Jung's "völkish agenda," his "promotion of völkish landscape mysticism," his "possible völkish elements," "the darker völkish nuances in Jung's transcendental theories," his "nakedly völkish" metaphors, all part of the "proto-Nazi Volkism" that clings to Jung's Germanic culture. As one who only recently traded in her Volkswagen (for a Honda!), I guess I can't defend Jung against these charges either, though there have been ample books, I think, that have.

Until I read this book, I never quite realized how much point of view is *everything*. So, okay, it's a cult. I've been had. I want my money back for Thomas Moore's *Care of the Soul*, for Clarissa Estes' *Women Who Run With Wolves*, for Hillman's *Re-Visioning Psychology*, for everything from Ginette Paris' *Pagan Meditations* to von Franz's *Puer Aeternus*, and especially for all my Joseph Campbell books. I'll never be fooled again. Richard Noll in the meantime ought to take a look at a Grateful Dead concert. Now *there's* a cult.

Book Reviews

Case, Margaret H., ed. *Heinrich Zimmer: Coming Into His Own.* Princeton: Princeton UP, 1994. Pp. 148, illustrated.

Zimmer was a great scholar of Indian art and culture who was an associate of Jung at the Eranos Conferences in Ascona. These essays, by Maya Rauch, Herbert Nette, William McGuire, Wendy Doniger, Gerald Chapple, Kenneth G. Zysk, Matthew Kapstein, Mary F. Linda, and posthumously by Zimmer himself are from a conference held at Columbia University in 1990:

"The Zürich lake has no lotus flowers and I have never seen Dr. Jung waving flowers in his hands. He taught me by pouring a generous drop of gin into a glass of lemon-squash I had in my hand. We were standing together at the Buffet in the Zürich Club, after I had my first lecture in his presence on Hindu yoga psychology. I was rather excited about this privilege to meet the man who after my opinion knew more about the human psyche than other men alive. So I was eager to get his criticism and asked him naively what was his opinion about the Hindu idea of the transcendental Self, indwelling man, underlying his conscious personality as well as the vast depth of the unconscious including the archetypes. But, without so much as disclosing his lips, while from the bottle in his right hand he poured the gin, with the forefinger of his left he persistently pointed to the rising level of the liquid in the glass, until I hastily said, "Stop, stop, thank you." [from Heinrich Zimmer, "The Impress of Dr. Jung on My Profession"]

Miller, Patricia Cox. *Dreams in Late Antiquity.* Princeton: Princeton UP, 1994. Pp. 273.

The most scholarly and rewarding book to date on ancient dreams, their psychology and symptoms, their images and history:

"The Synesian view that imagination is the basis of human consciousness was part of a widespread disposition in late antiquity concerning the construction of meaning. The idea of the imaginal basis of consciousness came to expression particularly when the issue concerned human knowledge of a divine or spiritual register of the real, that is, in the context of a desire to probe the depths of the visible. To offer just a few examples: Plutarch remarked that the gods speak in poetic circumlocutions, in image and metaphor; Philo spoke of tracking the scent of the divine through symbols and dreams; Plotinus said, "Everywhere we must read 'so to speak,'" suggesting that human speech about its access to the invisible world must always carry within it a metaphoric caution; Porphyry wrote that what is dark, obscure, and resistant to shaping comes to expression as a "shadowing forth in form"; Synesius, indeed, thought that the riddling unclarity of dreams constituted their wisdom, forcing us to do the hard work of interpretation without which no life is well-lived."

Lingis, Alphonso. *Abuses.* Berkeley: University of California Press, 1994. Pp. 268.

Lingis, a Professor of Philosophy at Penn State, is the most *sensuous* philosopher alive today. His specialty seems to be the philosophy of eros (*Foreign Bodies, Libido: The French Existential Theories, Excesses: Eros and Culture,* are some of his other books). *Abuses* ranges from Machu Picchu to Manila, and takes the reader on a fascinating tour of these cultures' human bodies as American culture is in the process of literally changing them from the shapes they originally were:

"One night during Carnival, there was a Michael Jackson look-alike...The same height, same huge eyes, infantile nose, thin lips and gleaming teeth, same cleft chin, same radiant, wild, vulnerable, wanton look...One couldn't help staring to try to see some details he had kept for himself: no, none...Michael Jackson himself is a product of plastic surgery. This Carioca has wiped away forever his own face to wear the face of a gringo who had wiped away forever his own face...I imagined Michael Jackson now redoing everything--dying his skin, having the surgeon build a broad-nostrilled nose, thick lips--and down in Rio this Carioca undergoing the same metamorphosis. I imagined them meeting. They would not be mirror images of one another. Michael Jackson could never be at ease with him. It would be black magic, macumba to him..."

Geuter, Ulfried. *The professionalization of psychology in Nazi Germany.* Tr. Richard J. Holmes. Cambridge: Cambridge UP, 1992. Pp. 335.

Rather than being banished and outlawed by the Nazi government, Geuter shows how professional psychology rose in stature during the 1930s and 40s. Jung gets only one mention in this exhaustingly documented study, and not—repeat, *not* as a sympathizer, but because his typology was ideologically *unsuitable* to racism. All you who want more professional recognition and institutional legitimation take note:

"...the profession conformed, compromised, and took the chances that offered themselves and made alliances so as to provide practical opportunities for psychologists. There was no incompatibility between their professional interests and the interests of the power centers. Professionalization was possible in a dictatorship."

Shay, Jonathan. *Achilles in Vietnam.* New York: Atheneum, 1994. Pp. 246.

A sensitive reading of Homer's *Iliad* by a psychiatrist for the Boston Department of Veteran Affairs Outpatient Clinic, relating the epic to Vietnam veterans' Post-Traumatic Stress Disorder:

"The Iliad opens with an interrupted fragging. When Agamemnon orders that Achilles' prize of honor be seized...Achilles has his sword halfway out of its sheath before the goddess Athena intervenes..."

THE JUNG CULT

Origins of a Charismatic Movement

RICHARD NOLL

In this provocative reassessment of C. G. Jung's thought, Richard Noll boldly argues that such ideas as the "collective unconscious" and the theory of the archetypes come as much from late nineteenth-century occultism, neo-paganism, and social Darwinian teachings as they do from natural science.

Noll sees the break with Sigmund Freud in 1912 not as a split within the psychoanalytic movement but as Jung's turning away from science and his founding of a new religion, which offered a rebirth ("individuation") surprisingly like that celebrated in ancient mystery cult teachings.

According to Noll, Jung consciously inaugurated a cult of personality centered on himself and passed down to the present by a body of priest-analysts extending this charismatic movement, or "personal religion," to late twentieth-century individuals. This is a fascinating book that is certain to spark heated debate.

" . . . [a] fine work of scholarship. . . ."—*Library Journal*

Cloth: $27.95 ISBN 0-691-03724-8

MYSTERIA: JUNG AND THE ANCIENT MYSTERIES

Extracts from the Collected Works of C. G. Jung

Selected, edited, and introduced by RICHARD NOLL

In this Mythos series original paperback, Richard Noll presents selections from writings, seminars, and conversations of C.G. Jung that demonstrate Jung's fascination with ancient gods and rituals. Noll uses these primary sources to explore the evolution of some of Jung's most significant insights.

Mythos Series

Paper: $14.95 ISBN 0-691-03647-0
Due January 1995

Not available from Princeton in the Commonwealth except Canada

ANALYTICAL PSYCHOLOGY SOCIETY
O F   W E S T E R N   N E W   Y O R K

The listing below gives selected titles, as well as presenters. Time, place, and costs are included in the complete program, which is printed triannually.

INDIVIDUATION IN COLOR
a lecture by
Paul Kugler, Ph.D.

**KUNDALINI YOGA:
JUNG'S 'JOURNEY TO THE EAST'**
a lecture by
Sonu Shamdasani, M.A.

**INNER CREATIVITY AND
CHANGE AT MIDLIFE**
a workshop with
Aryeh Maidenbaum, Ph.D.

DREAMS THAT TRANSFORM
a lecture by
Aryeh Maidenbaum, Ph.D.

**AN INTRODUCTION TO
CLINICAL PICTURES**
a seminar with
Paul Kugler, Ph.D.

**THE ARCHETYPES OF
PSYCHOLOGICAL TYPES**
a lecture with
John Beebe, M.D.

**PSYCHOLOGICAL TYPES:
A WORKSHOP BASED ON
A NEW MODEL**
a workshop with
John Beebe, M.D.

The Analytical Psychology Society of Western New York, founded in 1976 as a not-for-profit, membership-supported organization, focuses on studies and concerns in analytical and archetypal psychology. Membership is open to the public; dues are tax-deductible. Benefits include reduced prices for books, workshops, classes, and lecture series.

**For further information, write to: Analytical Psychology Society
of Western New York • 100 Coniston Road • Buffalo NY 14226-4660
or call (716) 854-7457**

What's been happening?

Spring 53 (Pagans, Christians, Jews) featured Jung's secret initiation into the mystery cult of Mithraism, James Hillman on "How Jewish is Archetypal Psychology?" Plus Ethnic Cleansing, Oracles, Jung's "Amfortas Wound," Disability, and Vampires.

Spring 54 (The Reality Issue) had Wolfgang Giegerich on killing for consciousness, David Miller on Animadversions, Edward S. Casey on Reality, plus articles on Typology, Islamic anti-Jungians, the Communitarian Self, Automatic Writing, and Hillman's updating of "Alchemical Blue."

Spring 55 (The Issue from Hell) is still smoking from Sheila Grimaldi-Craig's "Whipping the Chthonic Woman," as well as articles on "The Children of Hell," "Giving Voice to Hell," *Degeneration*, "Reading Jung Backwards," and more.

Spring 56 (Who Was Zwingli) brought James Hillman back "Once More into the Fray" to take on Wolfgang Giegrich, plus Ronald Schenk on Meaning, Benjamin Sells on Ethics, David Miller on Joseph Campbell. Plus Archaic Mind, Policing the Unconscious, Jung's *Zarathusthra* Seminar, and the first Index to *Spring* in years!

M.A. & Ph.D. Programs in Psychology and Mythological Studies

PACIFICA Graduate Institute, situated in the Santa Barbara foothills, offers unique Master's and Doctoral degree programs in Psychology and Mythological Studies, which examine archetypal motifs that infuse the psyche and culture.

ঙ PSYCHOLOGY

Pacifica's psychology programs are built on the conviction that the science of psychology is enhanced immeasurably by the study of literature, art, and mythology. The Institute offers a Ph.D. degree in Clinical Psychology and an M.A. degree in Counseling Psychology, both with degree specialization in Depth Psychology.

Recognizing the importance of cultural diversity, Pacifica also has an Overseas M.A. program in Counseling Psychology, which includes extended sessions in Greece and Hawaii.

ঙ MYTHOLOGY

Pacifica's innovative program in Mythological Studies explores world sacred traditions, symbolism, and ritual in light of the concepts of archetypal and depth psychology. The content of this sequential M.A./Ph.D. program is appropriate for adult students who are writers, artists, educators, religious leaders, managers, and others who wish to integrate mythological themes in their creative careers.

ঙ RESIDENCE & RESOURCES

Students journey from all points in the country to participate in Pacifica's graduate programs, and are in residence on campus each month for three-day retreat sessions.

The Joseph Campbell Archives & Library, the James Hillman Collection, and soon the Marija Gimbutas Archives & Library, along with the special holdings of the Institute's Graduate Research Library, provide a distinctive combination of resources for students and visiting scholars.

PACIFICA
GRADUATE INSTITUTE
Site of The Joseph Campbell Archives and Library
249 Lambert Road
Carpinteria, California 93013
(805) 969-3626 Fax (805) 565-1932
CANDIDATE FOR ACCREDITATION
WESTERN ASSN. OF SCHOOLS & COLLEGES

SPRING PUBLICATIONS

Our Titles Bare All

Michael Ventura writes in his briskly selling *Letters at 3AM*: "That's why sex play can be so intense: it follows the basic forms of ritual, it enacts the metaphor. Religious fundamentalists hate pornography not because pornography is evil, but because it's a rival; pornography is a form of religious fundamentalism." (247 pp., 0–88214–361–1)

In *Dark Eros: The Imagination of Sadism*, noted author Thomas Moore (*Soul Mates, Care of the Soul*) declares: "Like Sade we can say, if pornographic images appear spontaneously, then they must have a place. The very fact that they have such a claim on us, whether we feel their compulsion or are passionate in our distaste for them, demonstrates their power and suggests necessity." (200 pp., 0–88214–365–4)

Moved by a Reformation-era religious altarpiece, Jungian analyst Eugene Monick says in *Evil, Sexuality, and Disease in Grünewald's Body of Christ* that "there is no abundant life without sexuality—no life at all, in point of fact. There is no sexuality without disease." (189 pp., 0–88214–356–5, foldout color plates)

And Jungian analyst Jan Bauer enters the love-and-sex debate from a different angle in *Impossible Love—or Why the Heart Must Go Wrong*: "Wrong love has changed the course of history more often than wrong sex." (207 pp., 0–88214–359–X)